★

LONG MAY SHE WAVE

A Graphic History
of the American Flag

★

Kit Hinrichs
& Delphine Hirasuna
Photography
by Terry Heffernan

★

1○

Ten Speed Press
Berkeley/Toronto

★

CONTENTS

THE FLAG IN AMERICA'S DAILY LIFE
GERARD C. WERTKIN
DIRECTOR,
AMERICAN FOLK ART
MUSEUM

★

It was just over fifty years ago that I served for a term in the color guard of my Brooklyn, New York, grade school. Once a week, for assembly, all the boys of Public School 131 were asked to wear blue pants, white shirts, and red ties. I no longer remember how the girls dressed, but I assume it was also in patriotic red, white, and blue. We gathered together in the auditorium for exercises that invariably included the recitation of the Pledge of Allegiance and the singing of "America." As young as we were, those of us who had the honor of escorting the flag down the central aisle of the large hall did so with a sense of responsibility. Our teachers taught us that the flag deserved to be handled with the greatest of ceremony and care. If we marched with the special pride of young children, we also did so with the disquieting knowledge that any mistakes would be interpreted as signs of disrespect. I do not recall any horseplay; we were an earnest lot as we marched in step before our classmates.

I find myself surprised at the extent to which the flag was a presence in my childhood. Its display on national holidays was nearly universal in the Brooklyn of my youth, if not from the apartment building in which my family and I lived, then certainly from the front porches of the private houses that lined nearby streets. It excited my young imagination to see the repetitive colors and patterns of flags fluttering in the breeze from one street to the next. In contrast, I am not as aware— at least consciously—of the presence of the flag in the daily life that I now lead. Of course, it still stands as the preeminent national symbol, its very colors deep with meaning. Seeing it raised to the strains of the national anthem at the Olympic Games is a thrilling sight. For me, it was no less exhilarating

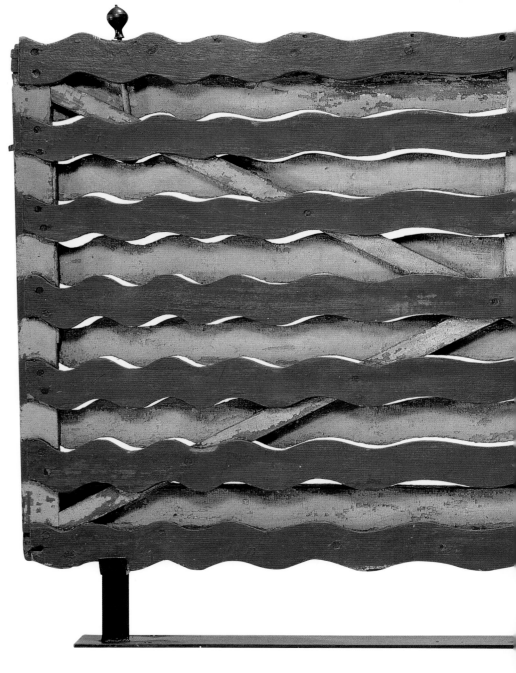

to see the flag unfurled atop the new building now being completed for the American Folk Art Museum in New York, a sure sign that the building had reached its full height.

As director of the New York American Folk Art Museum, I am regularly and happily reminded of the ubiquity of the flag in our visual culture. Some of the most engaging objects in the museum's collection are based wholly or in part on the Stars and Stripes: a remarkably diverse assortment of nineteenth- and twentieth-century quilts, needlework samplers, trade signs, whirligigs, weather vanes, even a sprightly megaphone. Each bears the red, white, and blue of its maker's national pride and identification as an American. Works of folk and vernacular art have

Flag Gate, New York State, Circa 1876, Collection of the American Folk Art Museum, New York

always been receptive to symbolic references to the nation—the image of liberty, the bald eagle, and Uncle Sam, for example, all figure prominently in American folk art—but only the flag seems to capture the full essence of America. Perhaps that is why its desecration is the ultimate expression of protest.

In 1962, soon after the American Folk Art Museum was established, it acquired its first object, the now famous *Flag Gate*, which once graced the entranceway to the Darling family farm in Jefferson County, upstate New York. It is one of my favorite works in the museum's collection. Researchers believe that the gate was created in 1876 in celebration of the centennial of American independence. Rather than painting a flat, motionless banner, its gifted maker sought to suggest that the flag was blowing in the wind through the use of curvilinear stripes. It is at once a utilitarian object, a statement of national identity, a commemoration of a moment in history, and a work of art. It underscores the profundity of patriotism as an impulse in American life.

We are fortunate that Kit Hinrichs has chosen to share his American flag collection through the pages of this volume. The flag is here presented in an extraordinary array of celebratory, ceremonial, political, commercial, and artistic settings, its power and appeal as a graphic image and an American icon given fresh and renewed emphasis. There is something comfortably familiar about this symbol that we call Old Glory, even in settings that may be new or surprising to us. But something else becomes increasingly clear as we study the images in this splendid book. Is it not Old Glory we turn to when we need to recall our common purpose as a people?

The American flag is but a piece of cloth decorated with stars and stripes, yet people have loved it, hated it, sworn allegiance to it, fought for it, and died for it. To millions of people, it is the embodiment of all that the United States stands for—its values, ethics, strengths, and foibles. The most recognizable national symbol in the world today, the American flag is so familiar that people think of it whenever they see the combination of red, white, and blue.

This makes it all the more interesting that the design of the original Star-Spangled Banner was decided without fanfare and for very practical reasons. Fighting for independence from Britain, the rebelling colonies urgently needed a way to identify their meager military possessions and naval ships. "Please to fix upon some particular Colour for a flag—& a Signal, by which our Vessels may know one another," Colonel Joseph Reed, George Washington's military secretary, asked naval contractors in a letter dated October 20, 1775. Although Colonel Reed suggested using the then well-known Green Tree Flag, the shortage of such flags left ship captains to agree on their own signal banner when sailing in common waters.

It was not until 1777 that the Continental Congress finally adopted an official standard in response to a request by an Indian named Thomas Green. Green sought a flag to

A GRAPHIC HISTORY OF AN AMERICAN ICON

★

★

1777

THIRD MARYLAND FLAG
Although many variations of the Stars and Stripes existed during the Revolutionary War, the thirteen-star wreath banner carried by the Third Maryland Regiment is often identified with this period.

★

take "to the chiefs of the nation" that would assure their safe passage when traveling on missions for the Continental Army. He included three strings of wampum, which signified a diplomatic gesture requiring a reciprocal effort. A flag for safe passage was critical to the Oneida Indians, who had provided pivotal support to the American cause and had suffered a heavy toll that cost the lives of about a third of its people. On June 14, 1777, eleven days after receiving Green's communiqué, the Continental Congress hastily responded: "RESOLVED: that the flag of the United States be thirteen stripes, alternate red and white; that the Union be thirteen stars, white in a blue field representing a new constellation."

The sketchy wording of the flag resolution suggests that Congress did not deliberate long on details, but instead treated the matter as just one of many resolutions on the agenda that day. The Founding Fathers left much undefined, including the size and number of points on each star, their arrangement on the blue field, and the width of the red and white stripes. As a result of this vagueness, flag makers did pretty much as they pleased, arranging stars of varying sizes, five-pointed and otherwise, in concentric circles, staggered rows, larger star patterns, geometric shapes, and random order.

JULY 1903
S M T W T F S
          1 2 3 4
5 6 7 8 9 10 11
12 13 14 15 16 17 18
19 20 21 22 23 24 25
26 27 28 29 30 31

AUGUST 1903
S M T W T F S
                1
2 3 4 5 6 7 8
9 10 11 12 13 14 15
16 17 18 19 20 21 22
23 24 25 26 27 28 29
30 31

"STRONGEST IN THE WORLD"

THE EQUITABLE
LIFE ASSURANCE SOCIETY OF THE U.S.
LIKE THE FLAG, GIVES SURE PROTECTION.

A BIT OF AMERICAN HISTORY.— OUR FIRST UNION FLAG (JAN. 2ND, 1776). (OVER.)

The liberty that the Continental Congress afforded flag makers was partly due to the fact that a national flag was not considered as important as the regimental colors of the militia or the Great Seal of the Republic. Its use was limited primarily to military holdings and naval vessels. Continental newspapers did not even bother to report passage of the flag resolution until the fall of 1777.

How the members of Congress arrived at a star-spangled banner of red, white, and blue is unknown, but one can see the influence of regimental flags in the design. A blue canton bearing thirteen stars graced both the flags of New Hampshire's Green Mountain Boys and the Continental Rhode Island Regiment. Boston's radical revolutionary group, the Sons of Liberty, had earlier adopted a red-and-white "stripes of rebellion" banner. The stripes reappear in the Continental Colors, also known as the Grand Union Flag, that bore a design of thirteen stripes, alternately red and white, with a blue field in the upper-left-hand corner bearing the red cross of St. George of England with the white cross of St. Andrew of Scotland.

The Continental Colors remained in general use throughout the colonies from 1775 until the flag resolution of 1777. The British crosses were likely dropped to avoid suggesting a hope for reconciliation under the Crown.

Although romantic lore often credits a Philadelphia seamstress named Betsy Ross with making the first Stars and Stripes banner, substantial evidence points to Francis Hopkinson of New Jersey, a signer of the Declaration of Independence, as the creator. Hopkinson was a commissioner on the Continental Congress's Navy Board when the flag resolution was adopted, and would have logically been involved in what was considered a naval matter. He also had a keen interest in heraldry and participated in the design of the Great Seal of the United States. Records show that in 1780, Hopkinson billed the Continental Congress for the equivalent of twenty-four dollars in public wine, in part for the flag design. Congress refused on the grounds that he "had not been the only one to work on the project" and because "individuals already receiving a salary from Congress should not try to charge the public more for 'these little assistances.'"

Even after the Revolution was won, Congress paid little attention to the nation's official banner. When Kentucky and Vermont were admitted to the Union in 1794, it was agreed to represent them on the flag by expanding the number of stars and stripes to fifteen, although at least one congressman complained that such an alteration was "a consummate piece of frivolity" that would cost sixty dollars for each ship in the merchant fleet.

This fifteen-star version inspired Francis Scott Key to write "The Star-Spangled Banner" after witnessing British warships steadily bombard Fort McHenry one night during the War of 1812. On the back of an envelope, Key scribbled his awe at seeing the Star-Spangled Banner through the "rockets' red glare" and "by the dawn's early light." In 1816, the poem was set to the tune of a popular English drinking song, "To Anacreon in Heaven," and its singing contributed to the cultural mythology surrounding the flag.

By 1818, the plan to represent each state with its own star and its own stripe proved unwieldy. With five new states

★

WELCOME HOME PIN
This button celebrates the release of American hostages held in Iran for four hundred forty-four days.

★

admitted into the Union that year and other territories vying for admission, it was clear that the broad stripes would soon become pinstripes. Balancing practicality and equality, Congress decreed that the flag revert back to thirteen horizontal stripes, alternating red and white, symbolizing the original thirteen colonies, with each state represented by a single star. Each star would be added on the Fourth of July following the date of admission to the Union.

The frequent addition of new stars—twenty-eight between 1818 and 1912—meant that the American flag was

★ FREE EDUCATION BADGE ★

★ ICE CREAM MOLD ★

★ TOY SOLDIER ★

★ BUTTERFLY WING COLLAGE ★

GOD BLESS AMERICA

★ CARVED RAZOR ★

hardly a static symbol. Like the nation itself, it was growing and ever changing. During the nineteenth century, new states were being admitted with such frequency that practical flag makers left gaps on the canton so that new stars could be stitched into place.

The average citizen, however, continued to view the nation's flag as primarily a military standard until the Civil War fostered a flag cult among those who sought to preserve the Union. The Stars and Stripes became a rallying symbol, particularly after secessionist troops bombarded Fort Sumter on April 12, 1861. The victory led Confederate Secretary of War L. P. Walker to

★

WORLD WAR I PIN
Volunteers raising
funds for Liberty Loans
during World War I
wore lapel buttons.

★

predict that the Confederate flag would fly "over the dome of the old Capitol at Washington before the first of May."

Outraged Northerners reacted by raising the Star-Spangled Banner in every town and village. Union nurse Mary A. Livermore recalls the sight in her autobiography, *My Story of the War* (1889): "Flags floated from the roofs of the houses, were flung to the breeze from chambers of commerce and boards of trade, spanned the surging streets, decorated the private parlor, glorified the school-room, festooned the church walls and pulpit, and blossomed everywhere."

★ SEWING PIN CASE ★

★ RALLY SHIELD ★

FIRE DEPARTMENT CONFERENCE RIBBON

★ FLAG ANTIMACASSAR ★

★ AMERICA BUTTON ★

★ EAGLE AND FLAG FAN ★

★

THE STAR-SPANGLED BANNER
Written by Francis Scott
Key during the War of
1812, the poem was
first published under the
title, "Defense of Fort
McHenry" and was set to
the tune of a popular
English drinking song.

★

Reverence for the flag intensified into a civil religion with the sight of the Stars and Stripes accompanying men going off to war and draping the coffins of fallen soldiers. Yankee mothers even taught their daughters to make small flags—sometimes called Bible flags because they were tucked into the family Bible—to foster patriotic devotion. The Star-Spangled Banner resonated emotionally with citizens who displayed their loyalty and affection by integrating the flag motif into everyday life.

This cult of the flag continued after the Civil War ended and gained strength with the celebration of America's Centennial in 1876. To mark the anniversary of the nation's birth, the United States hosted its first world's fair in Philadelphia, where it exhibited innovations and achievements that boasted of the country's progress and promise for the future. Reinvigorated with national pride, Americans adorned all kinds of objects with images of the Stars and Stripes.

This patriotic momentum grew stronger in the closing decade of the nineteenth century as veterans groups and women's hereditary societies embraced the flag as the vehicle for teaching

★

EMBROIDERED CLOTH
Early women's
magazines printed
embroidery
patterns featuring
patriotic themes
for their readers'
enjoyment.

★

INTRODUCTION ★ ★

young people proper moral code, patriotism, and respect for cultural institutions. In 1892, the veterans group of the Grand Army of the Republic (GAR) successfully lobbied to require flags to be raised on all schoolhouses and pushed to have them flown in churches. That same year Francis Bellamy wrote "The Pledge of Allegiance" for a popular magazine called *The Youth's Companion* to mark Columbus's discovery of America. Reprinted on thousands of leaflets, The Pledge of Allegiance was sent out to schools nationwide for children to recite at Columbus Day festivities. Many schools continued this practice even though Congress did not officially recognize The Pledge of Allegiance until 1942.

Politicians and merchants, quick to capitalize on the cult of the flag, appropriated the popular icon for their own purposes. Politicians printed their campaign slogans and portraits on flag banners, and merchants unabashedly wrapped their wares in flag packaging and made the Stars and Stripes part of their trademark. By the late 1890s, the Stars and Stripes could be seen on everything from pincushions

CODE OF ETIQUETTE
It was not until 1934 that a code of conduct defined the appropriate way to display the American flag. As a public service to immigrants applying for citizenship, the Veterans of Foreign Wars distributed this pamphlet.

and pillowcases to clown costumes and pickled pork. In the absence of official flag guidelines, flag makers, commercial enterprises, and private citizens were free to follow their own fancy—and did. Patriotic societies charged that the blatant commercial exploitation of the flag was cheapening the nation's most revered symbol and lobbied to protect it from rampant desecration. Soon more than two hundred flag committees were formed on local, state, and national levels to define proper flag usage by advertisers, merchants, and politicians. During the first quarter of the twentieth century, Congress approved a code of flag etiquette and a series of detailed design standards. Today the official flag adheres to strict design guidelines and is uniform in appearance and presentation.

More than a century without official rules, however, has yielded a wealth of exuberant and unbridled creative interpretations of the national banner. Fascinating for what they reveal about the culture and history of the United States, these ephemeral flag objects and artifacts are their own genre of folk art and a unique part of the American heritage.

CANDY MOLD
This stamped mold, measuring 3.5" x 2.5", features a World War I doughboy marching off to battle.

THE DESIGNER'S EYE: A COLLECTOR'S PASSION FOR THE AMERICAN FLAG

★

★

Often when my design colleagues learn that I collect American flags, they are intrigued by my interest. I suspect that some wonder, "How varied can the flag be? You've seen one American flag and you've seen them all." Only after I have shown them my collection (which now numbers some three thousand objects), do they appreciate the richness of the topic.

My own fascination with the American flag began as a kid growing up in Los Angeles. My family's only heirloom

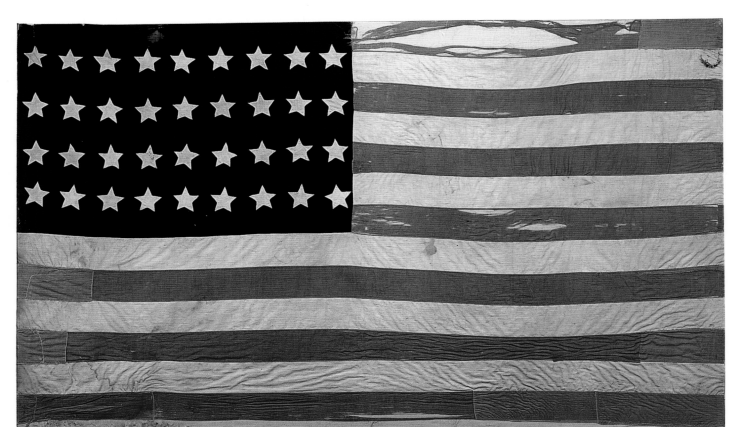

★

This 4' x 6' Civil War flag is the cornerstone of Kit Hinrichs's American flag collection. The thirty-six-star, hand-sewn wool flag is a family heirloom created in Ohio in 1865 by his great-great-great aunt Ida Pepperkorn.

★

was a tattered and patched thirty-six-star Civil War flag sewn by my great-great-great aunt Ida Pepperkorn in 1865. My mom considered it so precious that she kept it wrapped in tissue in a sturdy department-store box, and she stored it in the safest place in the house—under her bed. When I was in first grade, my mom allowed me to take this keepsake to school for show-and-tell. Needless to say, Aunt Ida's flag received more ooohs and aaahs than the run-of-the-mill pet rabbit, horned toad, and bird's nest. That was my proudest moment in first grade.

★ THE COLLECTION ★

Twenty years later, my parents asked me to be the family caretaker of this coveted flag, and I had it framed and hung it in a prominent place in my first New York apartment, where it became a natural conversation piece whenever anyone visited.

My interest in the Stars and Stripes could have ended there, but as a designer, I am in a profession where creating graphic symbols is an important aspect of my work. It was a symbol I couldn't leave alone. Designers are continually challenged to come up with visual icons that evoke immediate recognition, emotional power, and universal meaning. We talk buzzwords and use terms like brand building, establishing corporate identity, and creating a clear visual language. By any standard, the American flag has brand value that every corporation would envy. In terms of pure graphic strength, the Stars and Stripes is distinct and compelling. People recognize it even in snippets of color and pattern.

But the American flag is not only a symbol that everyone recognizes. It is also one to which everyone, not only Americans, has a personal and often visceral response. Over the past two hundred years, people have expressed their feelings toward the country through the flag. They have used it to legitimize their cause, whether a product or a political campaign. They have shown their displeasure over a political position or a military activity by their vilification of it. And they have proclaimed their patriotic pride through it, even when reticent to express themselves in actual words.

When I view my collection as a whole, I am fascinated by the many forms and interpretations the Stars and Stripes have taken over the decades. I have found flags frozen in ice cream, made of broken tile and cemented in a wall, carved in tree trunks, baked in cookies, molded in Jell-O, etched in granite, made of pressed flowers, and sprinkled with red, silver, and blue glitter by a Haitian-American immigrant. My design colleagues Bob Brunner and James Biber even used the shape of a waving flag as their inspiration for the design of the official millennium time capsule for the U.S. government. Through this parade of objects and imagery, I've learned a lot about the social milieus from which the various flag interpretations emerged. Trying to find out who the Captain Rodgers of the "Corea" flag was led me to read up on Civil War ironclads, obscure battles, and military traditions. Noting that certain materials did not exist prior to a given date prompted me to research manufacturing methods and design styles. It is not just the flag as a designed object that has intrigued me. It is the rich history that surrounds it, too.

For me, the collector's passion is in the joy of discovery—in sorting through piles of stuff at antiques fairs and flea markets and finally unearthing a new and wonderful iteration of the Stars and Stripes; in learning about how people lived and thought in another time; and in deepening my appreciation of the independent spirit and resourcefulness of the true "designers" of the flag, the American people.—*Kit Hinrichs*

THE COLLECTION

THE FLAG IN

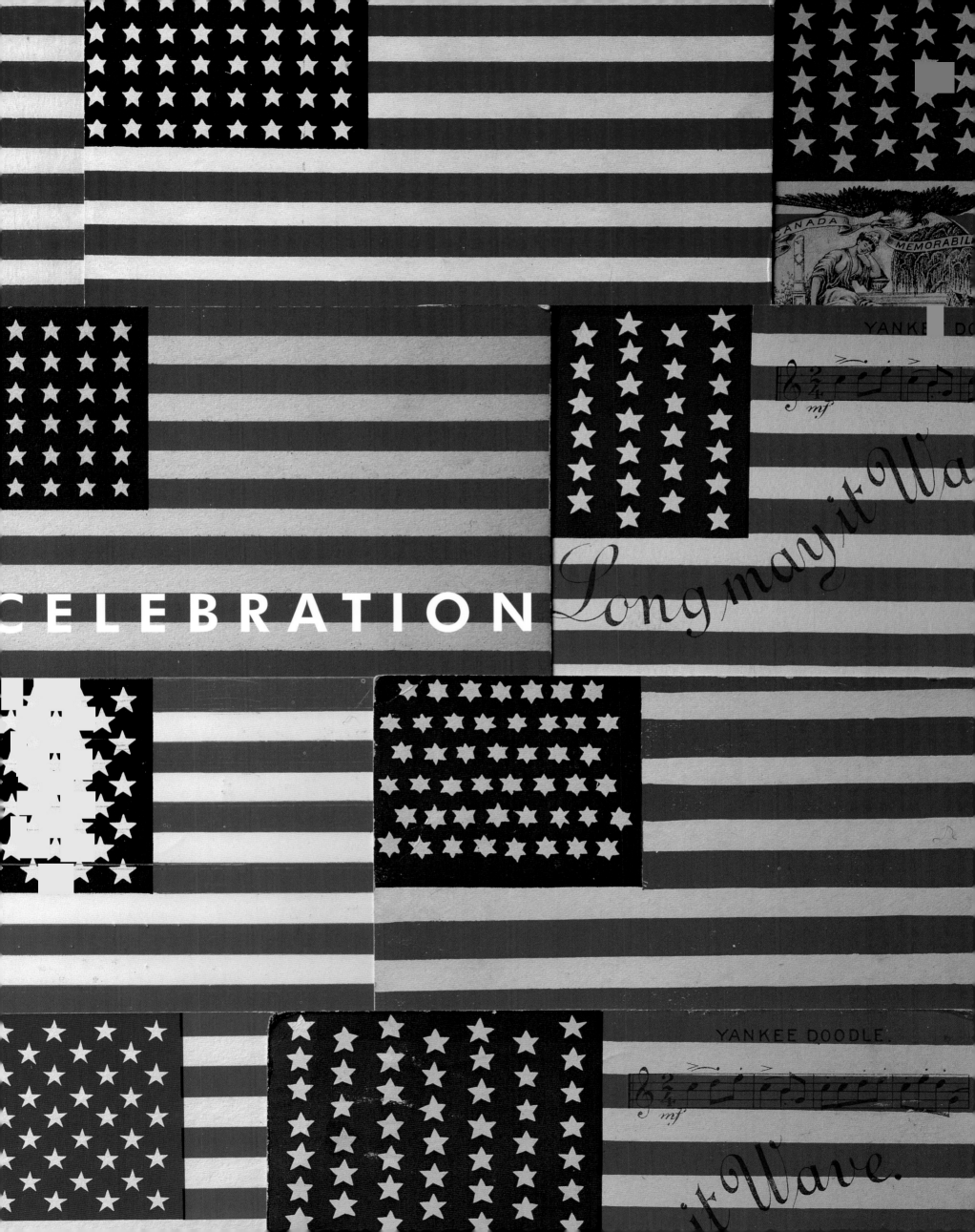

★

LIVING FLAG

1917

USA

BLACK-AND-WHITE
PHOTOGRAPH

10" x 8"

Living flags were all the rage at the start of the twentieth century, but arguably none was bigger than the one created on the parade ground at the United States Naval Training Station in Great Lakes, Illinois. Ten thousand cadets participated in the forming of the human flag.

★

★

LIVING FLAG POSTCARDS

1909

USA

PRINTED PAPER

3.5" x 5.5"

★

★

"Solid as the Oak"
Pillow Cover

Circa 1900

USA

Embroidered Cotton

20" x 20"

Needlework patterns that
could be traced from women's
magazines or purchased at
departments stores have long
incorporated the Stars and
Stripes into the design,
particularly in the early
twentieth century.

★

★

Patriotic Shield
Nesting Box

Circa 1900

USA

Cardboard and Cotton

2.75" x 2.75" x 1.25"

★

Mr Miller.
Elks Home. Springs, Colo.
Colorado

Oct

Lodge last night Bro Van Vechten presented
the Lodge with the flag as requested by you
and upon motion it was ordered that a vote
of thanks be tendered you for the same and
the Secretary was directed to write you of
this action and to assure you of the appreciation of the members of the Lodge.

Dear

At the meeting of the

and Brother:

White Mountains, N.H. Mount Pleasant House.

Mason & Hamlin Pian

TO THE
CARNIVAL GROUNDS.

Parade Corner. Newport, R.I.

BUILDING
DECORATIONS

Trimming public
buildings for patriotic
occasions was a special
skill that was much
in demand in the early
twentieth century.
Professional bunting
decorators traveled
around the country
taking commissions
from towns, civic
organizations, and
political groups.

★

★

FLAG CANCELLATION MARK

CIRCA 1890

USA

STAMPED PAPER

3" x 4"

In the late 1800s, the
cancellation mark used by
the U.S. Postal Service
depicted a full waving flag.
By the 1920s, the mark had
been abbreviated to only
the waving stripes,
still used today.

★

★ CHRISTMAS ORNAMENT ★   ★ UNCLE SAM HAT BROACH ★   ★ MONEY CLIP ★

★

SCOUT KNIFE

CIRCA 1940

USA

INLAID PLASTIC AND STEEL

3.75" x 1" x .5"

Loyalty, patriotism, and duty
to country have long
been important aspects of
Boy Scout training, and
Stars and Stripes figure
prominently in Scout
equipment and design.

★

★

"TO HELP BUY A FLAG"
FLAG PINS

CIRCA 1925

USA

PRINTED PAPER AND
METAL PINS

2.5" x 2.75"

To earn money to buy a
flag for their unit, Boy
Scout troops would receive
a free box of thirty flag pins
from a flag manufacturer
and sell the pins for ten
cents each. The three dollars raised from the sale
was enough to purchase a
three-by-five-foot flag.

★

★

LADY LIBERTY POSTCARD

CIRCA 1890

GERMANY

PRINTED PAPER

5.5" x 3.5"

A European postcard maker overprinted different flags on the same model to sell to different national markets.

★

★

LADY LIBERTY POSTCARDS

CIRCA 1910

GERMANY

PRINTED PAPER

3.5" x 5.5"

Pinup and patriotism merged in these Victorian-era postcards that depict Lady Liberty posing in front of the flag. Presented as the American ideal of womanhood, Lady Liberty models ranged from wholesome and youthful to matronly and prim to winsome and alluring.

★

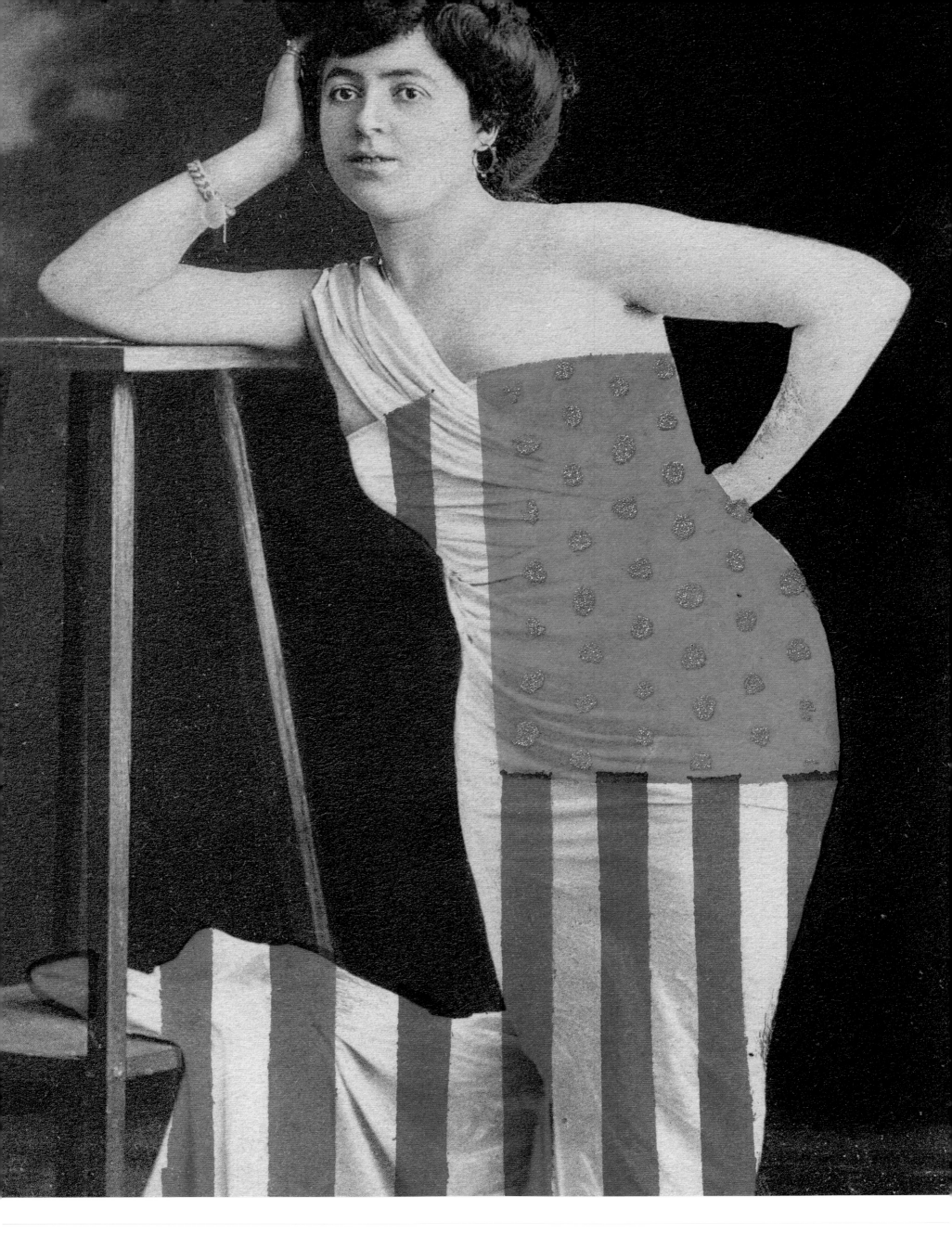

FLAG AND DOG
SHOTGUN SHELL CASE

CIRCA 1940

USA

WOOD, METAL,
AND LEATHER

10.5" x 9.5" x 3.5"

A one-of-a-kind piece,
this shotgun shell
case was lovingly inlaid
with hunting dogs
and the flag by an
amateur woodworker.

★

HOOD ORNAMENT

CIRCA 1915

USA

PUNCHED TIN,
WOOD, AND COTTON

3.5" x 7.5" x 7"

The car and the
airplane were both
recent inventions when
this pre–World War I
hood ornament was
made to fly gaily from
its mount on the
radiator cap.

★

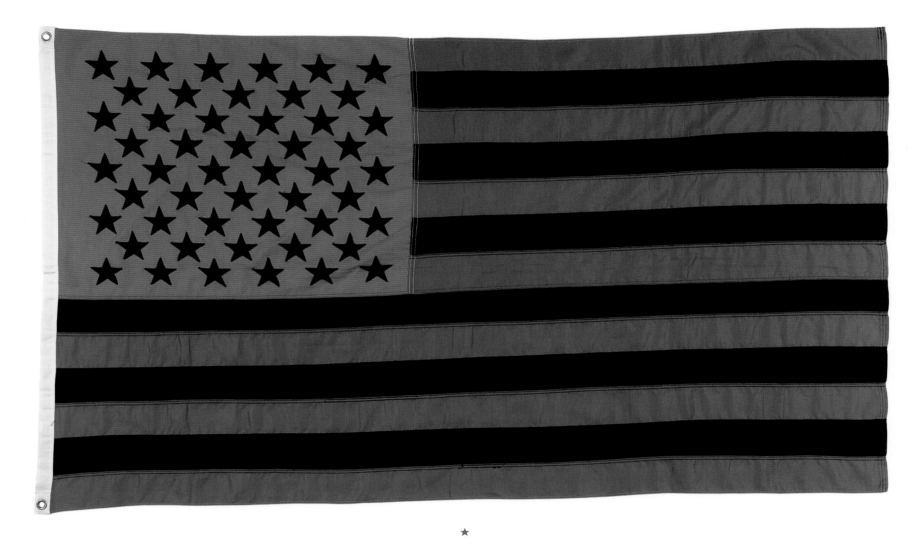

★

COMPLEMENTARY COLOR FLAGS / CIRCA 1960 / USA / COTTON / 30" X 60"

During the op art craze of the 1960s, a manufacturer created a flag set that relied on the optical effect that complementary colors can have on the human eye. Staring at the colored flag for thirty seconds and then quickly looking at the white flag, you can see an afterimage in red, white, and blue appear on the white flag.

★

★

WOVEN RIBBONS

Beginning in 1862, political ribbons began
featuring finely detailed words and
images thanks to a silk-weaving technique
called Stevengraph, invented by English
ribbon maker Thomas Stevens using
a Jacquard loom. The first Stevengraphs
appeared as bookmarks, and were later
followed by other formats such as postcards.
This selection includes Stevengraphs,
as well as traditional printed, stamped,
and embroidered ribbons.

★

★

UNCLE SAM
FOLDING FAN

CIRCA 1900

USA

PAPIER-MÂCHÉ AND
PRINTED PAPER

7.25" X 1.5"

Manufactured in Japan,
this novelty item takes
the shape of Uncle Sam,
and, when pulled, opens
out into a Stars and
Stripes fan.

★

★

Cigar fans have existed
for more than one
hundred years. This fold-
ing design also found
its way into papier-
mâché carrots and the
Statue of Liberty.

★

"Old Glory"

TRIBUTE TO THE·FLAG
By former Senator George F. Hoar

I have seen the glories of art and architecture, and of river and mountain. I have seen the sunset on the Jungfrau and the moon rise over Mount Blanc. But the fairest vision on which these eyes ever rested was the flag of my country in a foreign port! Beautiful as a flower to those who love it, terrible as a meteor to those who hate it, it is the symbol of the power and the glory and the honor of the millions of Americans.

33—OLD GLORY

THE AMERICAN ART WORKS
COSHOCTON, OHIO

Handed out by local merchants at patriotic celebrations, stick fans usually bore imagery on one side and the advertiser's message on the other.

★

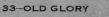

COMMERCE

★

CAMPBELL'S SOUPS
REPLICA TIN SIGN

1994

USA

PRINTED AND EMBOSSED TIN

11.5" x 16.5"

To celebrate its 125th anniversary in 1994, the Campbell Soup Company reissued the embossed tin advertising sign that it introduced in 1910. The original sign appeared during the height of the movement to stop commercialization of the nation's banner and aroused so much controversy that it was not used for long.

★

★

WHEATLET TRADING CARD

CIRCA 1900

USA

PRINTED PAPER

6.5" x 3.5"

At the start of the twentieth century, Uncle Sam was often featured as a product "spokesman" because he was viewed as a strong symbol of an emerging power and a proponent of American enterprise.

★

AAA Sign Co., Coitsville, Ohio

TOBACCIANA

Between 1890 and 1910, the American tobacco trust waged a major marketing war in an attempt to monopolize all forms of tobacco production—an effort that allowed the American Tobacco Company to control roughly 90 percent of the tobacco production in the United States and Europe by 1903. To woo smokers, the company offered all kinds of collectible premiums, including cigar "felts," cigarette cards, cigar bands, and decorated boxes. A favorite theme was the Stars and Stripes, which appealed to the consumers' sense of patriotism and reminded them that tobacco originated in America where the best tobacco products were still being produced.

★ PRESIDENTIAL CIGAR BANDS ★

★ CIGAR "LEATHER" ★

★ PATRIOTIC CIGARETTE "SILK" ★

★ TOBACCO "FELT" ★

Thousands of cigar and cigarette brands existed in the early twentieth century, so producers tried to win customers' loyalty by offering collectible give-aways. Promotional series such as the Presidential cigar bands and international flag series on cigar "felts," "leathers," and cigarette "silks" lured customers who wanted the complete set.

★ "BELLA" CIGARETTE CARD ★

★ CIGARETTE "SILK" ★

★ PRESIDENTIAL CIGAR BANDS ★

★

SUNLIGHT SOAP
PROMOTION

CIRCA 1890

GERMANY

LITHOGRAPH, EMBOSSED
AND DIE-CUT PAPER

7.75" x 4.25"

★

★

Until the nation adopted
an official code of flag
etiquette in 1934, advertisers
took enormous liberties with
how America's banner was
displayed. They arranged the
stars in different patterns,
wrote all over the flag, and
used it to tacitly endorse
everything from corn salve,
tooth powder, and soap
to playing cards.

★

★ ADVERTISING TRADE CARD ★

★ FLAG MANUFACTURER TRADE CARD ★

★ TOOTH POLISHER TRADE CARD ★

★ PLAYING CARDS TRADE CARD ★

★ SOAP TRADE CARD ★

★ CORN SALVE HAND BILL ★

★ BAR SOAP TRADE CARD ★

★ FERTILIZER TRADE CARD ★

PAGE 73

THE FLAG IN AR

AND FOLK ART

★

Tattooed Sailor

Circa 1930

USA

Sepia Photograph

5" x 3.5"

This is one of two "postcard" views of William Roy, whose body, from waist to neck and front to back, was tattooed with patriotic and nautical imagery.

★

★

"American Girl"

1990

USA

Black-and-White Photograph

13" x 12"

Jock McDonald's homage to the American woman was created with more than two hundred graphite flag impressions.

★

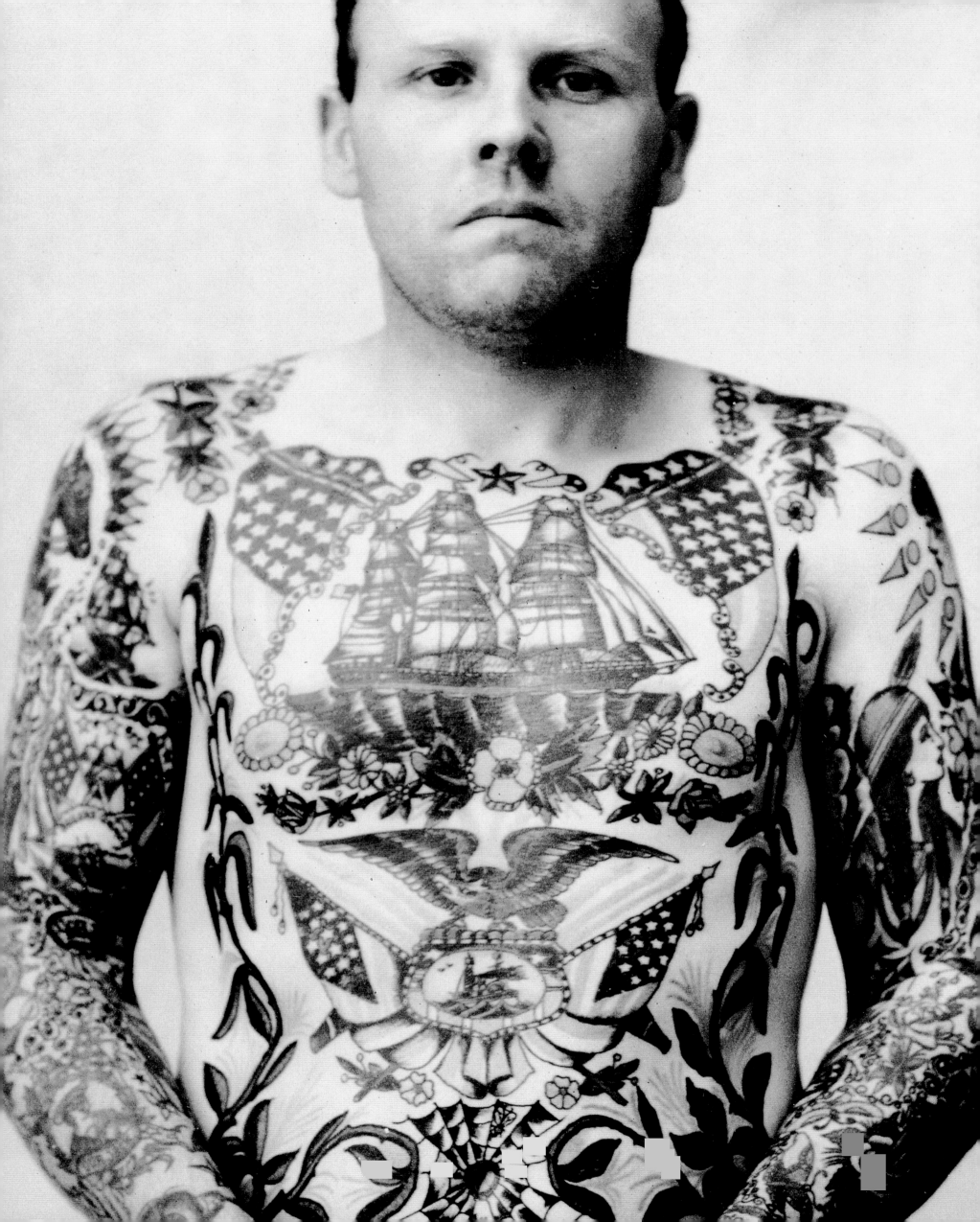

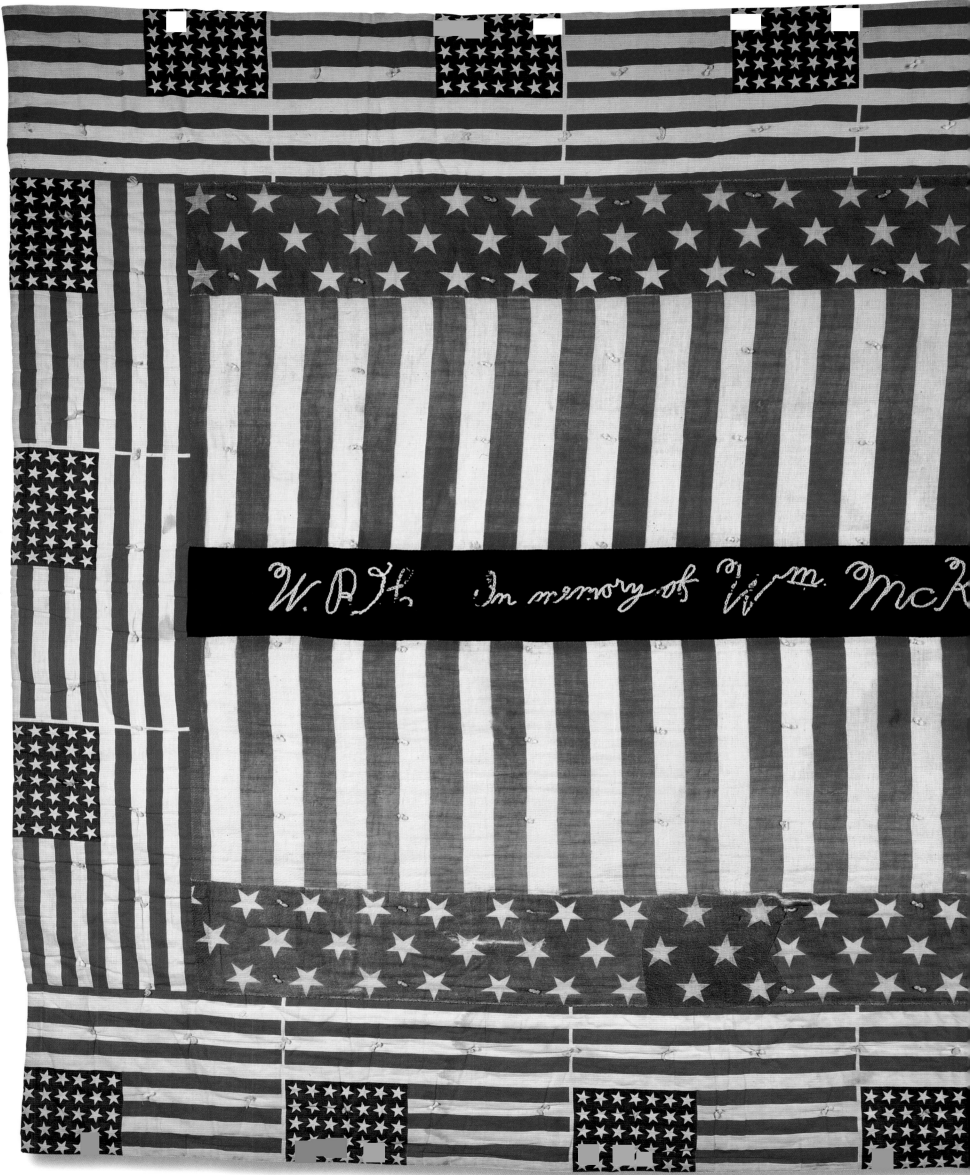

★

MCKINLEY QUILT

1901

USA

COTTON BUNTING

68" x 80.5"

This quilt was made
in memory of William McKinley,
who was elected president
of the United States in 1897,
and was assassinated by an
anarchist named Leon Czolgosz
in 1901. The initials W. R. H.
are that of the quilt maker.

★

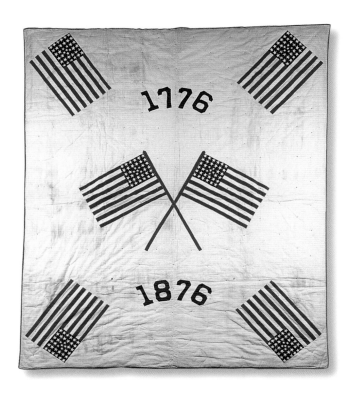

★

CENTENNIAL QUILT

1876

USA

COTTON

81" x 70"

Obviously created to mark
the nation's Centennial,
this quilt features thirty-six-star
flags, even though thirty-eight
states were officially part of
the Union at the time.

★

★

"Non-Melting Pot"

1976

USA

Serigraph on Paper

33" x 48"

Based in New York City, Italian-born product and graphic designer Massimo Vignelli created this Bicentennial flag out of ethnic newspapers circulating in New York. Through this work, Vignelli portrays an America that is not so much a melting pot, encouraging assimilation, but rather a place that tolerates and supports the coexistence of different cultures and opinions.

★

★ DANIEL PELAVIN / PROTO-COLOR ★

★ SANDRA MCHENRY / POLAROID ASSEMBLAGE ★

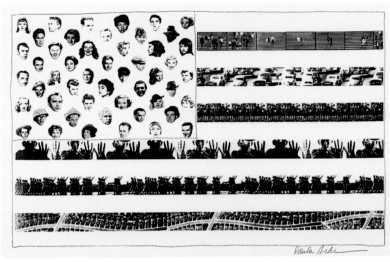

★ PAULA SCHER / MIXED MEDIA ★

★ TIM LEWIS AND ALAIN J. BRIERE / ILLUSTRATION BOARD ★

★ LINDA HINRICHS / GLASS BEADS AND BRASS RODS ★

★ REGAN DUNNICK / PASTEL ON PAPER ★

★ MARSHALL ARISMAN / COLLAGE OF PAINTINGS ★

★ DON SIBLEY / PAINT ON METAL ★

AIGA DESIGNER FLAG SERIES

In 1986, the American Institute of Graphic Arts (AIGA) invited ninety-six leading graphic designers and illustrators to interpret the Stars and Stripes in honor of the Statue of Liberty's one-hundredth anniversary. The submitted artwork reflected a cross-section of America with its diverse cultural, regional, and political points of view; pop culture interpretations; and historical perspectives. The AIGA reproduced the original art pieces in a book called *Stars & Stripes* (Chronicle Books, 1987) and auctioned them off at a gala event to raise funds for the nonprofit design organization.

★ ANTHONY RUSSELL / INK ON PAPER COLLAGE ★

★ EVERETT PECK / GOUACHE ON BOARD ★

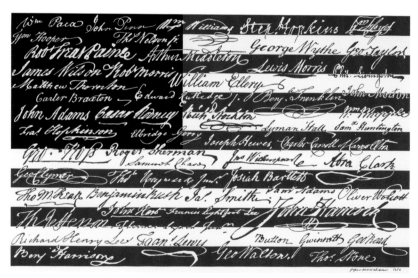

★ PIPER MURAKAMI / SERIGRAPH ★

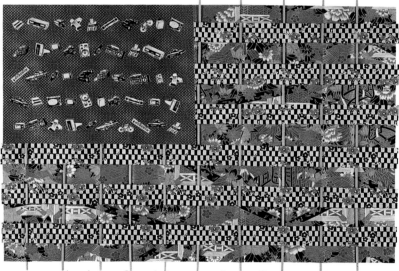

★ JOHN COY / JAPANESE PAPER COLLAGE ★

★ CONRAD JORGENSEN / PHOTOCOPY COLLAGE ★

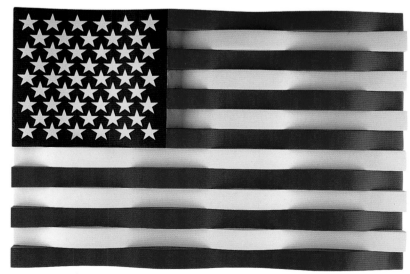

★ MIKE HICKS / ENAMEL PAINT ON WOOD ★

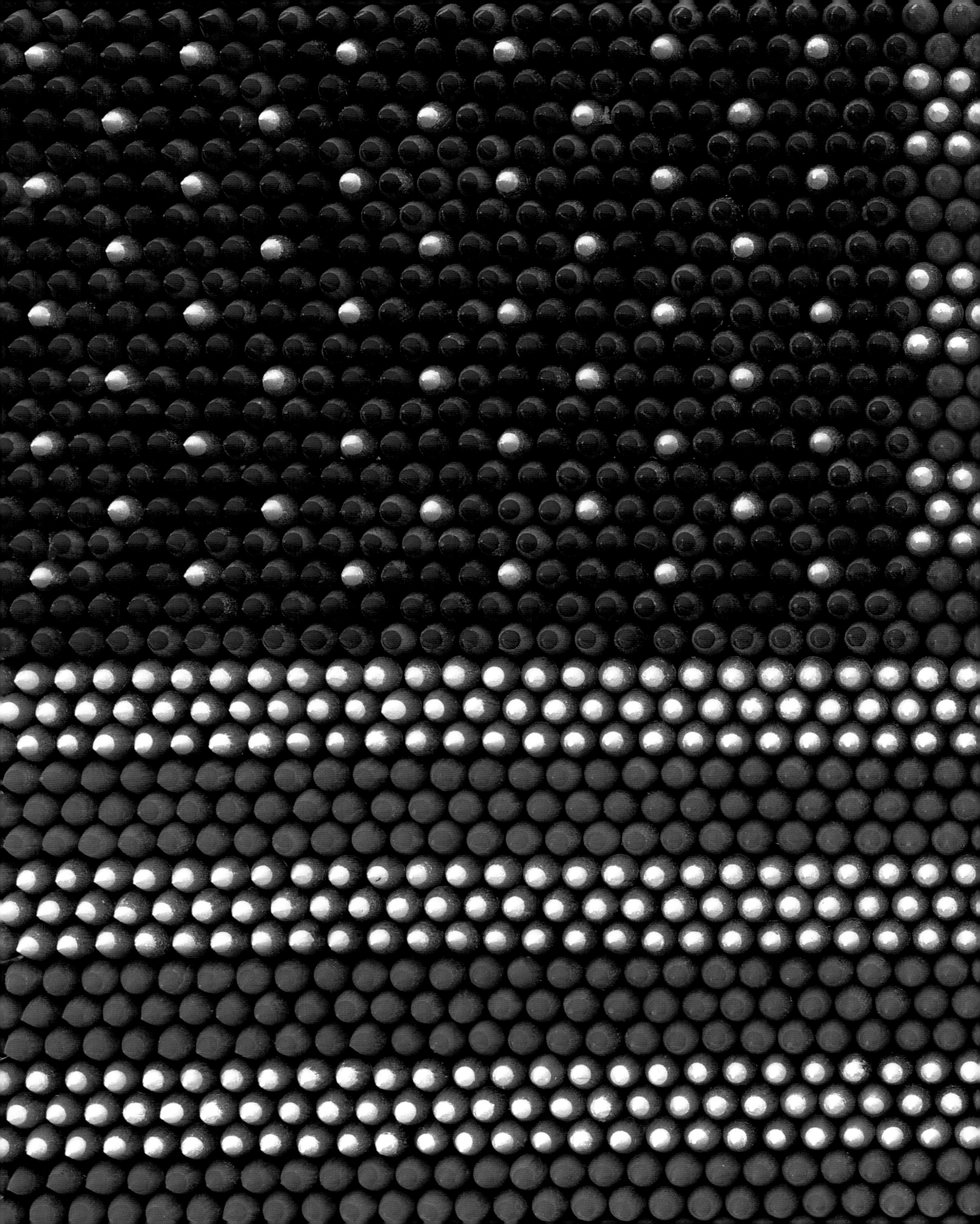

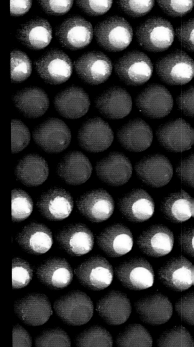

★

FLAG PENCIL ASSEMBLAGE

1986

USA

PRISMACOLOR PENCILS

12" x 18" x 2.5"

For the American Institute
of Graphic Arts exhibition
and auction in 1986,
Texas-based graphic
designer Chris Hill
created this original
piece out of twenty-four
hundred red, white,
and blue pencils.

★

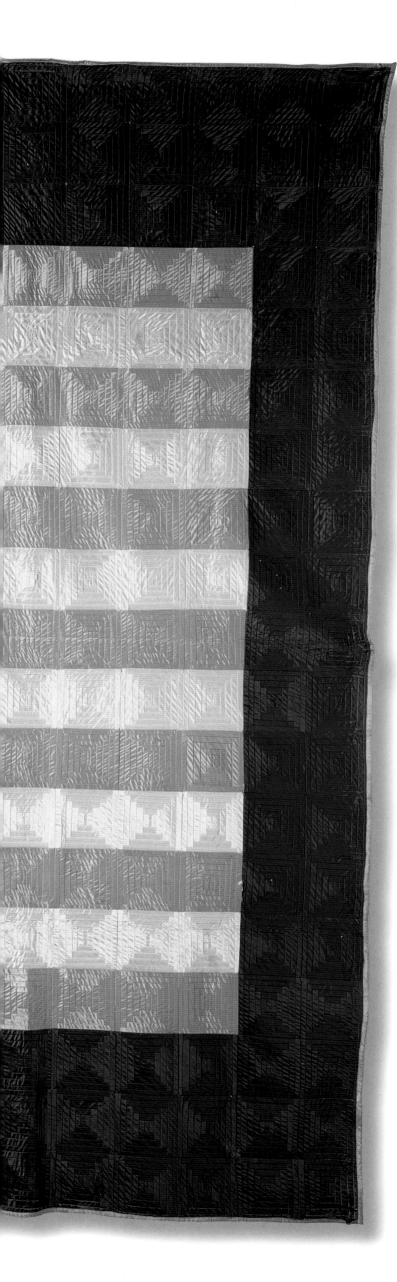

★

LOG CABIN QUILT

CIRCA 1910

USA

SILK

88" x 104"

Made by a ten-woman
sewing bee in Nevada,
this log cabin quilt once
hung in the offices of
the San Francisco chief
of police.

★

★

GREEK AND AMERICAN FLAGS

1939

USA

GLASS BEADS AND WOOD

14" x 11"

This homemade flag,
created from beads wired to
a painted vegetable crate,
celebrates the friendship
between Greece and the
United States and bears the
Greek inscription "liberty."

★

★

UNCLE SAM POSTCARD

CIRCA 1900

CHINA

INK, WATERCOLOR, AND
STAMP COLLAGE

5.5″ x 3.5″

Popular during the
early twentieth century,
the uniquely Chinese
art form of watercolor
and collage was used
to create this image
of Uncle Sam. Uncle
Sam's attire is exclu-
sively made out of
canceled U.S. stamps.

★

★

UNCLE SAM
MECHANICAL BANK

1978

USA

ENAMEL ON WOOD

18″ x 7″ x 3″

David and Susan Kirk
created this folk art
mechanical Uncle Sam
bank (his eyes recede
and his tongue extends
to receive coins) in
the late 1970s. David
Kirk has gone on to
create the Miss Spider
children's book series.

★

★ Salesman's Flag / 1912 / USA / Printed Buckram / 31.5" x 47.25" ★

★ Although this looks like a precursor to the paintings of Jasper Johns, it is actually a flag
salesman's sampler produced in 1912 to introduce the new forty-eight-star flag. ★

EAGLE AND FLAG
ARMY BLANKET
1914
USA
EMBROIDERED WOOL
82" × 60"

Aware that the United States would soon be engulfed in Europe's Great War, an American soldier, whose initials were E. E. H. embroidered this army blanket for his parents.

★

CHINESE EAGLE
CIRCA 1900
CHINA
SILK EMBROIDERY ON COTTON AND VELVET WITH A GLASS BEAD
22" × 20"

The advent of the Open Door Policy with China in 1899 encouraged trade between China and the United States. Intricately embroidered silk pictures, often with frames for photos, were popular with U.S. sailors, traders, and merchant seamen stationed or working in Asia. This art evolved into a thriving business in elaborately embroidered jackets for servicemen from World War I through Vietnam.

★

1980 THE 50TH ANNIVER
SARY OF THE WHITNEY M
USEUM OF AMERICAN ART

★

WHITNEY MUSEUM
FIFTIETH ANNIVERSARY POSTER

1980

USA

LITHOGRAPH ON PAPER

46.5″ X 30″

The American flag was a
popular subject for pop artist
Jasper Johns. He described
his fascination with the everyday images that surround us
as "things the mind already
knows." Johns uses two flags
from different eras to describe
the passing of time for the
fiftieth anniversary poster.

★

★

CROCHETED FLAG

CIRCA 1930

USA

COTTON

12.5″ X 23″

The forty-eight silk stars
are appliquéd in silk
to this hand-crocheted
folk-art flag.

★

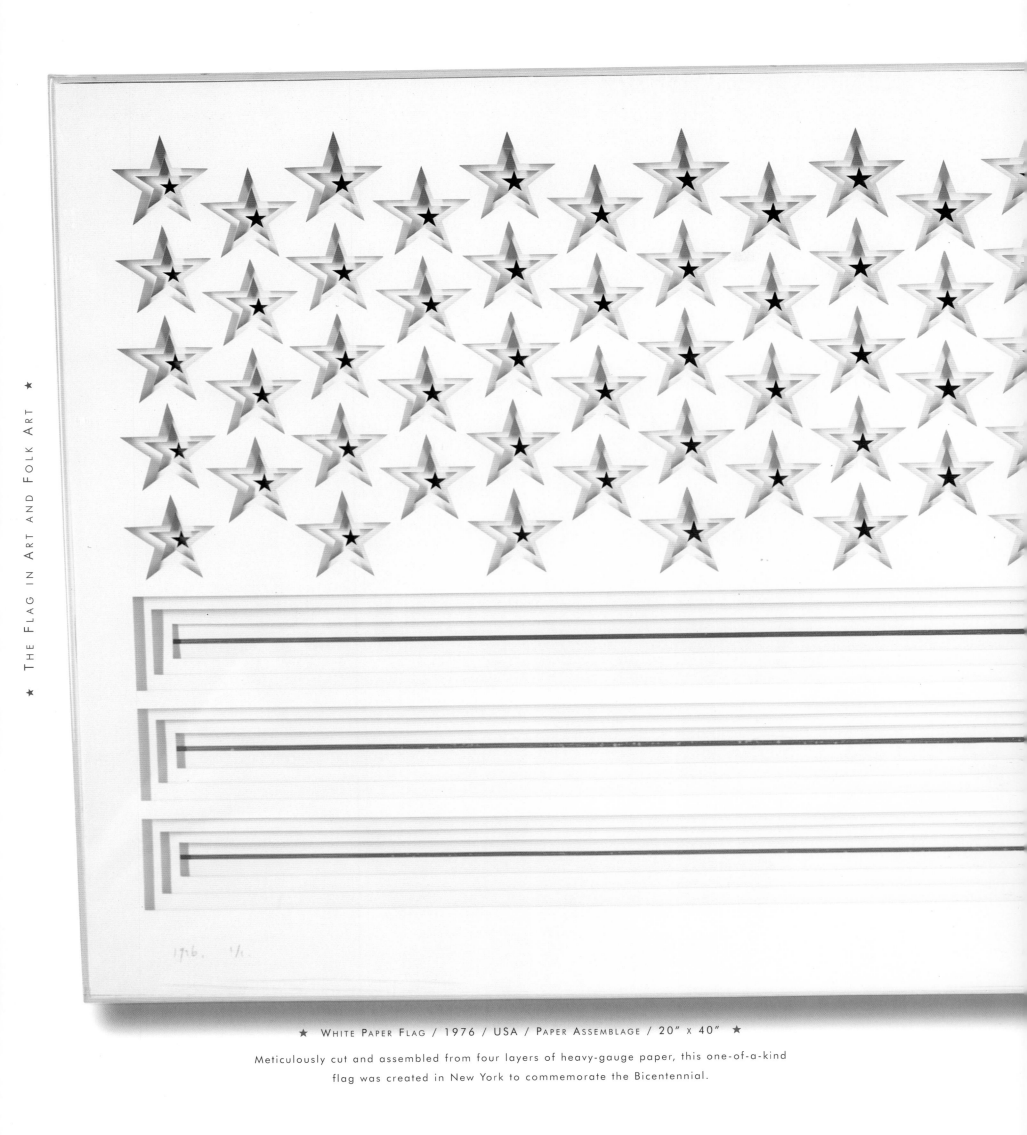

★ White Paper Flag / 1976 / USA / Paper Assemblage / 20" x 40" ★

Meticulously cut and assembled from four layers of heavy-gauge paper, this one-of-a-kind
flag was created in New York to commemorate the Bicentennial.

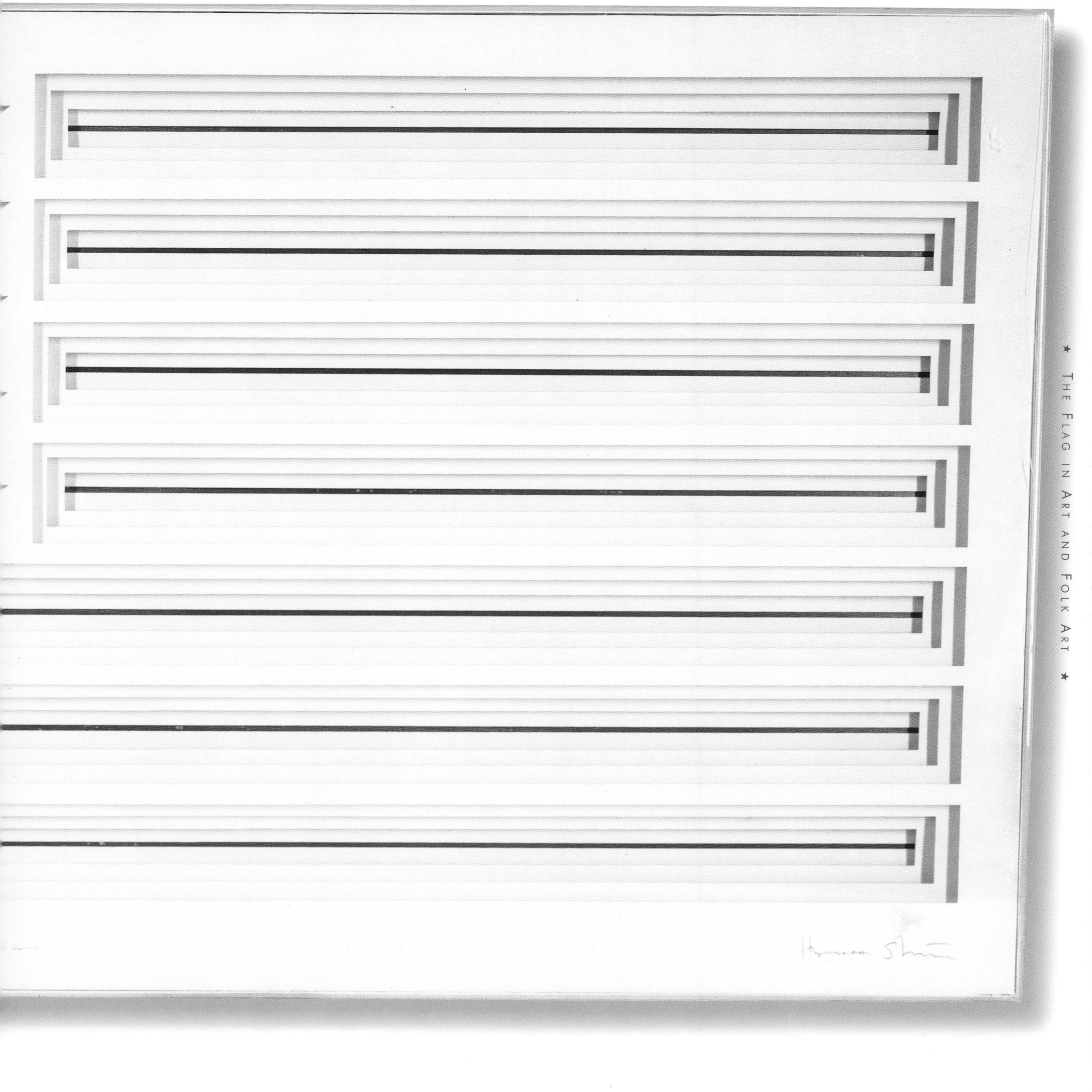

THE FLAG

AT PLAY

★

STARS AND STRIPES
BLOCKS SET

CIRCA 1925

USA

PAINTED AND STAMPED WOOD

6.75" X 9.25"

A commercially made
educational toy from the
1920s, this child's block set
presents the Stars and
Stripes on one side and the
alphabet on the other.

★

★

STAR PUZZLE

CIRCA 1920

USA

TIN AND CERAMIC BEADS

2.5" X 2.5" X .5"

★

★

FLAG DOMINOS

CIRCA 1880

USA

EMBOSSED AND
PAINTED WOOD

1" X 1.75" X .25"

★

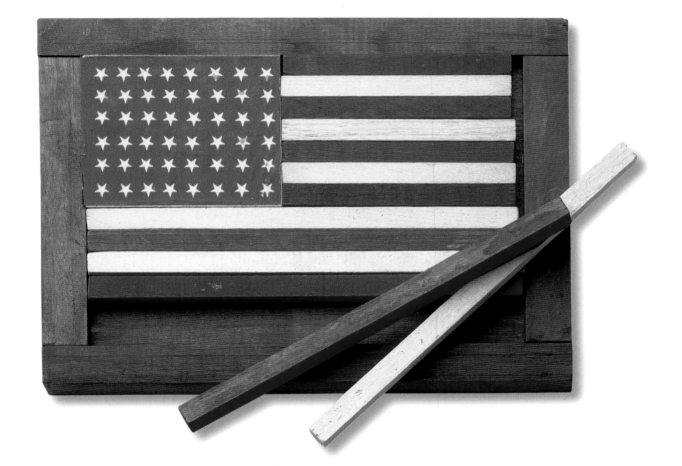

★

FLAG STIX PUZZLE

CIRCA 1930

USA

PAINTED WOOD
AND PAPER

5.5" X 7.5" X .63"

The Stars and Stripes
was just one of
dozens of national
flags that could be
created with Flag Stix.

★

★

HOMEMADE
LEARNING PUZZLE

CIRCA 1930

USA

PLYWOOD, METAL PEGS,
AND PLASTIC DRAWER
HANDLES

17.75" x 20.5" x 2.5"

★

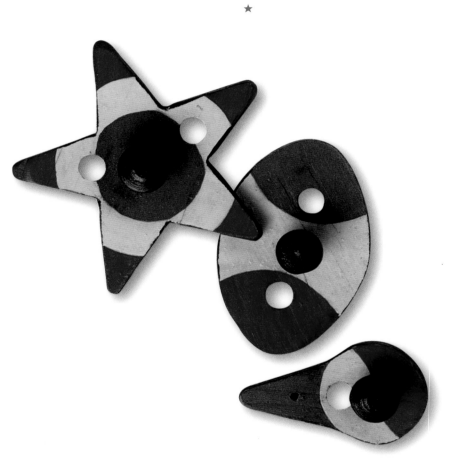

★

This homemade
puzzle game was
designed to teach a
young child how to
match sizes, shapes,
and colors.

★

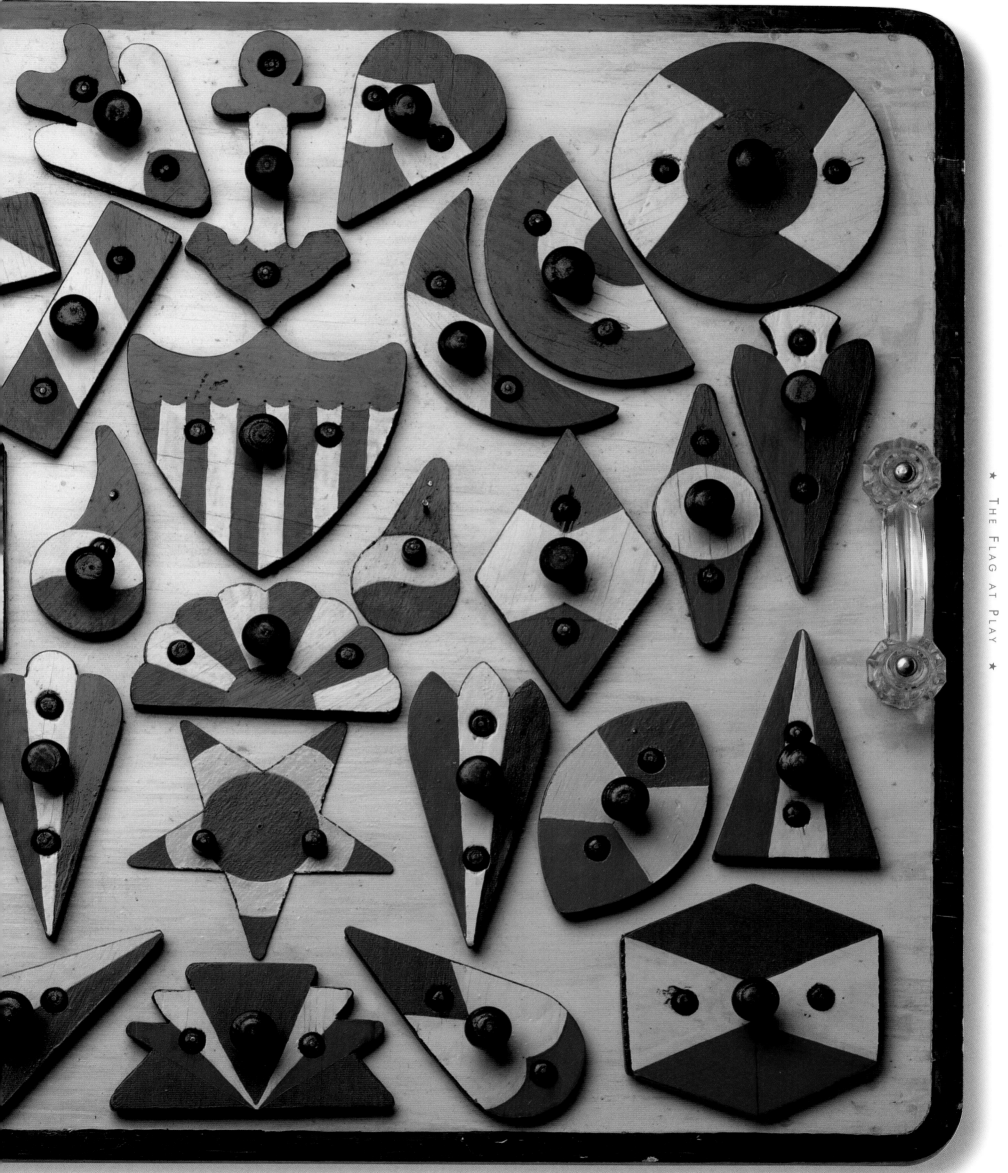

★

HANGING PARTY FLAG

CIRCA 1980

DENMARK

COLORED TISSUE PAPER

50" x 27"

This collapsible
die-cut tissue flag
expands from .75"
to 50" for home or
office Fourth of
July parties.

★

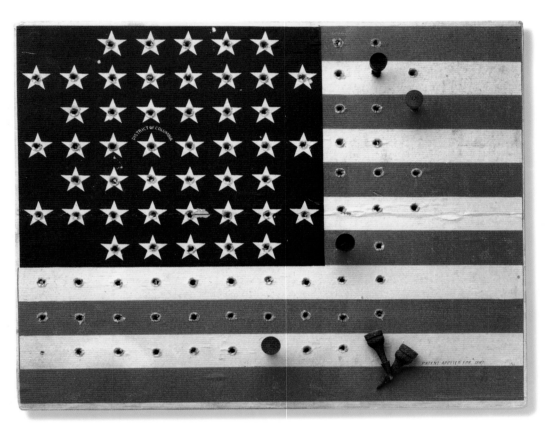

★

PEG GAME

CIRCA 1910

USA

PRINTED PAPER
AND WOOD

8.5" x 10.25" x .5"

★

TOY SOLDIER
FLAG BEARERS
METAL, CERAMIC, AND COMPOSITION MINIATURES

Not only a plaything but also a means to instruct boys in the military arts, toy-soldier sets have existed since the days of the Egyptian pharaohs. Virtually every set has included a flag bearer who embodied the nation's honor, carrying it into battle and serving as a rallying point for the troops. Over the centuries, toy soldiers have been cast from metal, carved out of wood, and made from composition (sawdust and glue), and then hand painted. Among collectors, the flag bearer is usually the most coveted soldier, both for the symbolism of his role and the intricate workmanship required in reproducing the flag. U.S. toy-soldier sets represent every conflict, from the American Revolution and Custer's Last Stand to the Gulf War, and every branch of the military.

★

★

WORLD WAR I SOLDIER

CIRCA 1920

USA

CAST LEAD

3.2" x 1.4" x 1"

★

★

DAN BOHLINE

CIRCA 1980

USA

ENAMEL ON LEAD

5.4" x 5.5" x 1.25"

★

★

TOTSIE TOYS

CIRCA 1920

USA

PAINTED METAL

2" x .75" x .2"

★

★

JONES/DIMESTORE

CIRCA 1930

USA

ENAMEL ON LEAD

3.75" x 1.5" x 1.4"

★

★

MIGNOT

CIRCA 1930

FRANCE

PAINTED LEAD

3" x 1.75" x .75"

★

★

DAN BOHLINE

CIRCA 1980

USA

PAINTED LEAD

7.25" x 1.75" x 1.5"

★

★

GREY IRON

CIRCA 1930

USA

PAINTED IRON

3.6" x 1.25" x .75"

★

★

BARCLAY

CIRCA 1930

USA

ENAMEL ON LEAD

3.5" x 1.25" x 1.5"

★

★

DAN BOHLINE

CIRCA 1980

USA

ENAMEL ON LEAD

6.5" x 1.75" x 1.5"

★

★

ELASTOLIN

CIRCA 1930

GERMANY

PAINTED COMPOSITION

7.5" x 5.2" x 1.25"

★

★

ELASTOLIN

CIRCA 1930

GERMANY

COMPOSITION WITH TIN

4.25" x 2" x .75"

★

★

TIRCO

CIRCA 1930

JAPAN

PAINTED COMPOSITION

8.5" x 2" x 2.5"

★

★

BARCLAY/PODFOOT

CIRCA 1950

USA

PAINTED LEAD

4.5" x 1.25" x 1.5"

★

★

MIGNOT

CIRCA 1930

FRANCE

PAINTED LEAD

4.75" x 1.5" x 1"

★

5.75″ x 1.5″ x .5″

Teaching love of God
and country was as
important as writing
and arithmetic at the
turn of the last century.
The Stars and Stripes
motif appeared on
everything from lunch
pails to slate markers
used for writing on
slate boards.

★

CARNIVAL DOLLS

CIRCA 1940

USA

AIRBRUSHED PLASTER

14.5″ x 4″ x 4.5″

American men and
women fighting overseas
were never far from
people's minds during
World War II. These
patriotic plaster
carnival dolls were
favorite prizes at
county-fair arcades.

★

PATRIOTIC
BED DOLL

CIRCA 1920

USA

CERAMIC, HAIR, SILK,
AND CANVAS

26.5" X 20"

Fine satins and brass
buttons were added
to this Lady Liberty
bed doll. These dolls,
which varied in theme,
were not meant to
be playthings. They
were instead used as
decorative accents
on beds.

★

VICTORY PLAYING CARDS

1942

USA

PRINTED PAPER

3.75" X 2.5"

Small, lightweight, and
inexpensive, playing
cards gave servicemen
and -women a brief
respite from the war.
Card decks usually
pictured patriotic
themes. Here, Hitler
and Mussolini are
the Jokers.

★

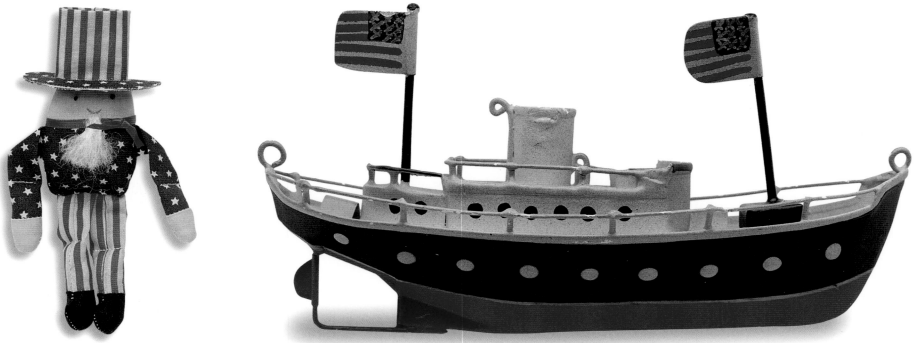

★ UNCLE SAM DOLL ★

★ HAND-PAINTED METAL BOAT ★

★ PARKER BROTHERS GAME OF FLAGS ★

★ FINGER TOP ★

★ PATRIOTIC DOLL ★

★ BICYCLE BELL ★

Mechanical tin toys
have been popular with
children for generations.
Manufactured in both
Japan and the United
States, patriotic icons
like Uncle Sam, American
soldiers, circus figures,
and Lady Liberty were
favorite subjects.

★

★ THE FLAG AT PLAY ★

U.S.A.

KUBL

SPAIN

JOSE

NAZIS MASSACRE 5% OF OCCUPIED E

U.S.A. MASSACRES 6.5% OF SOUTH VI

FOR CALCULATIONS & REFERENCES W

★ "Genocide Records!" Poster / Circa 1970 / USA / Printed Paper / 21.5" x 34.5" ★

URPASSES ALL THE GENOCIDE RECORDS!

KHAN MASSACRES 10% IN NEAR EAST

MASSACRES 10% OF AMERICAN INDIANS

STALIN MASSACRES 5% OF RUSSIANS

OPEANS AND 75% OF EUROPEAN JEWS

NAMESE & 75% OF AMERICAN INDIANS

TE TO: P.O. BOX 180, NEW YORK, N.Y. 10013

★

BENJAMIN HARRISON
HANDKERCHIEF

1888

USA

PRINTED SILK

20.5" x 19.5"

★

★

GROVER CLEVELAND
HANDKERCHIEF

1892

USA

PRINTED COTTON

19" x 19"

★

FOR PRESIDENT.
BENJAMIN HARRISON.
FOR VICE PRESIDENT.
LEVI P. MORTON.

AID FOR FREE SCHOOLS.

A.S. Rosenthal & Co. N.Y.

BENJAMIN HARRISON
HANDKERCHIEF
1888
USA
PRINTED SILK
22" x 20"
Campaign slogans
and political giveaways
proliferated in the
late nineteenth century
as presidential
candidates were forced
to wage a cross-
continental campaign
and as printing
technology became
more affordable.

THE FLAG IN POLITICS AND PROTEST

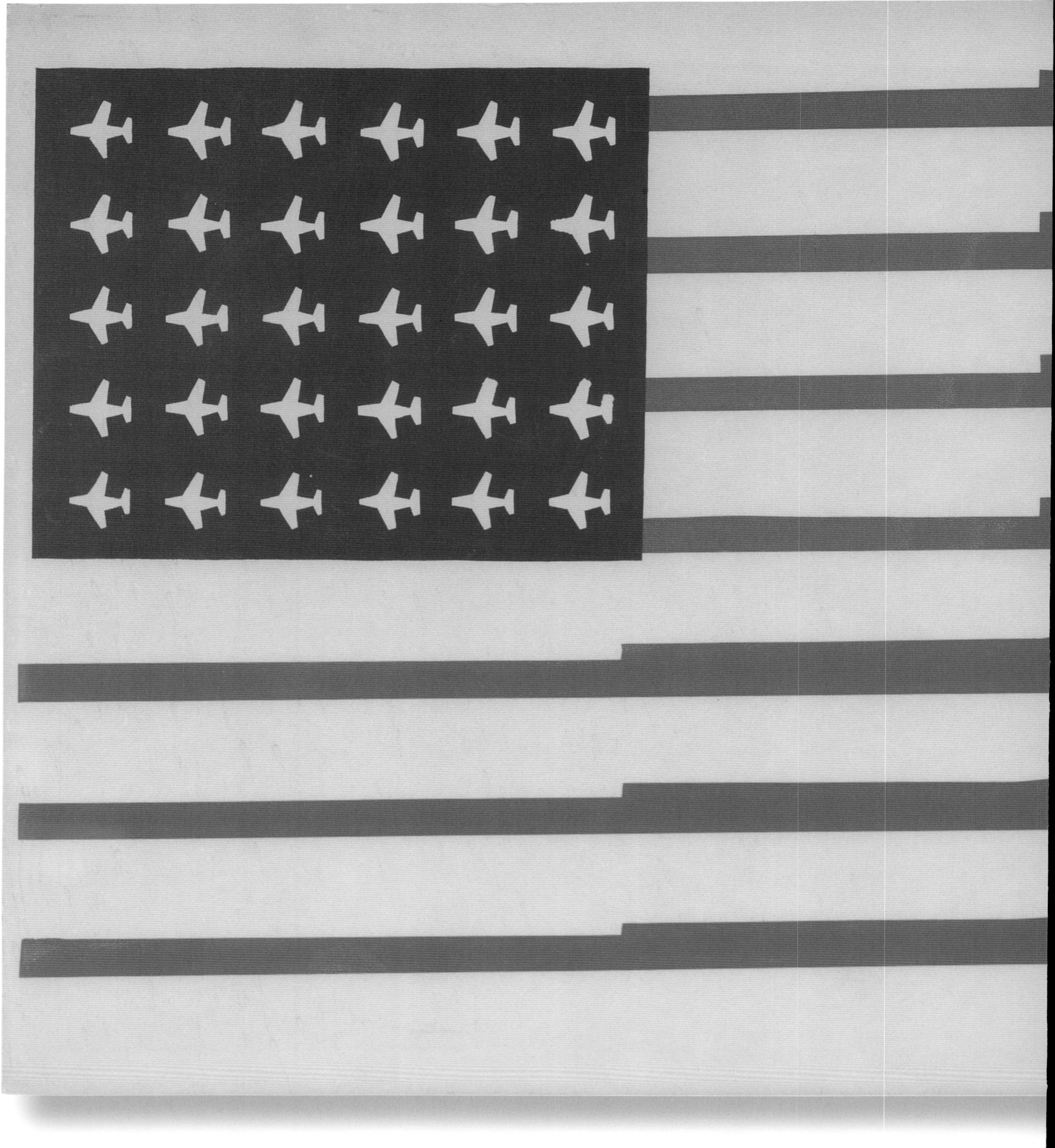

NJAMIN HARRISON

FOR VICE PRESIDENT

OTECTION.

EVI P. MORTON

★ Woven Door Mat / Circa 1970 / West Germany / Natural Fibers / 12" x 20.5" x .75" ★

★ During the Cold War, a West German manufacturer expressed its resentment of America's military presence in the country. ★

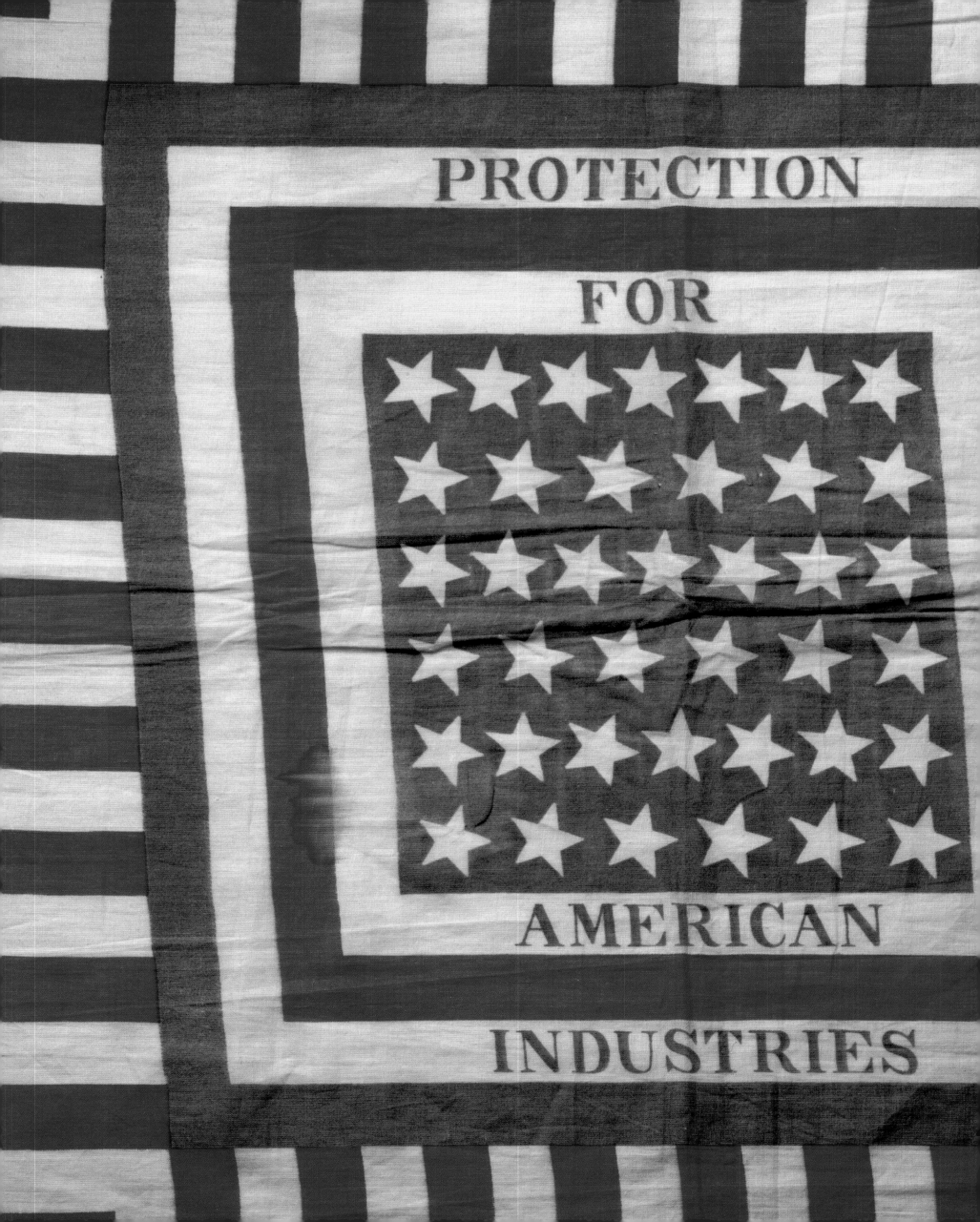

PROTECTION

FOR

AMERICAN

INDUSTRIES

★

"PROTECTION FOR
AMERICAN INDUSTRIES"
BUNTING

1880

USA

PRINTED CLOTH

24" x 24"

Bunting—cloth printed
with the Stars and Stripes
motif—was used
extensively to decorate
political rallies.

★

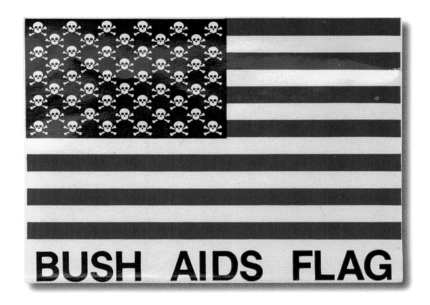

★

"BUSH AIDS FLAG" STICKER

1990

USA

PRINTED PLASTIC

3" x 4"

Protesting that AIDS
victims were dying
because of insufficient
research funding by the
George H.W. Bush
Administration, ACT UP
New York issued a
flag sticker with skulls
and crossbones in
place of stars.

★

Seymour Chwast
"End Bad Breath" Poster
1967
USA
Printed Paper
39" x 28"

Seymour Chwast played off the familiarity of Flagg's poster in creating a woodcut of Uncle Sam protesting the aerial bombing of Hanoi during the Vietnam War. The distorted use of stripes and red, white, and blue reinforces the sense that things are not as they should be.

★

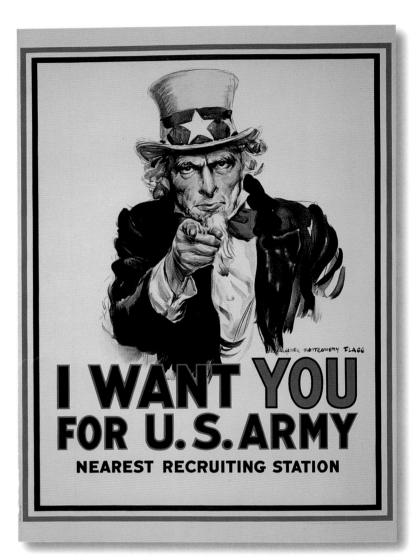

I WANT YOU
FOR U.S. ARMY
NEAREST RECRUITING STATION

★

"I Want You" Poster
1917
USA
Printed Paper
36" x 28"

One of the most recognized images of the twentieth century, this World War I recruitment poster was the work of James Montgomery Flagg, who used himself as the model for Uncle Sam.

★

End Bad Breath.

Flag Day, Saturday, Oct. 31.

The American Flag has been in the present campaign the emblem or insignia of national honor. Its influence has been for great good in the cause of a good people. Its display in many places has been potent in the advancement of the country's battle for the maintenance of its honor at home and abroad.

I therefore suggest that **Saturday, October 31**, all who intend to vote November 3d for the preservation of our national honor, for sound money and the advancement of our people's interests and general prosperity, display the national colors at their homes, their places of business and wherever they may be seen, in order that voters whose hearts are for their country may be strengthened in their purpose and those who are undetermined may the more patriotically and intelligently conclude how best to perform their duty as citizens.

M. A. HANNA,

CHICAGO, Oct. 17, 1896. *Chmn. Republican Natl. Com.*

SOUND MONEY · PROTECTION AND PROSPERITY.

★

McKINLEY AND HOBART
POLITICAL POSTER
1896
USA
PRINTED PAPER
16.75" x 23"

★

★

WILLKIE RHINESTONE PIN
1940
USA
METAL AND GLASS
2" x 1.25"

This rhinestone pin
promoted Wendell Willkie,
who ran and lost against
Franklin Roosevelt
in 1940.

★

MAY OUR GLORIOUS FLAG AND THIS "LUCKY STAR"
GUIDE YOU AND KEEP YOU WHEREVER YOU ARE.

PATENT PENDING

★

"INDIAN POWER"

1975

USA

SERIGRAPH ON PAPER

25" x 19"

Designer and *Graphis* magazine publisher B. Martin Pedersen boldly illustrates the diminishing power of the American Indian over the centuries in this limited edition print.

★

★

PEACE FLAG

CIRCA 1970

USA

PRINTED COTTON

33" x 58.5"

The American flag is so
graphically distinctive
that it remains recogniz-
able as the national
banner even when
protest groups have
substituted their own
symbol in lieu of
the stars.

★

★ PRESIDENT THEODORE ROOSEVELT COMMEMORATIVE POSTCARD ★

★ POLITICAL CAMPAIGN BUTTONS ★

★ BRYAN CAMPAIGN POSTCARD ★

★ FDR RIBBON ★

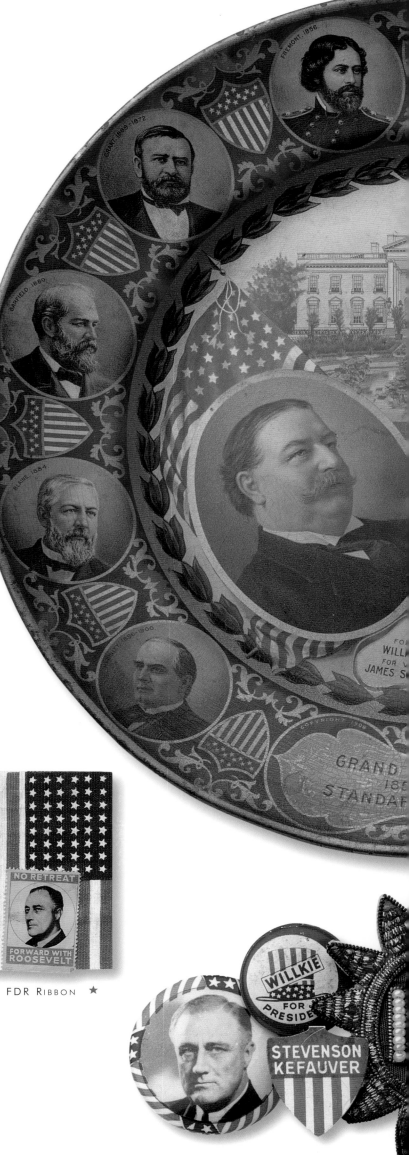

★ POLITICAL BUTTONS AND PINS ★

★ FDR RIBBON ★

ROOSEVELT

HUMPHREY — MUSKIE

NO RETREAT

FORWARD WITH ROOSEVELT

LET'S STAND BY THEM BOTH

★ POLITICAL CLICKER ★

ELECT JOHNSON

★ LBJ BANNER ★

FOR PRESIDENT

Wm. H. TAFT OF OHIO

A Stainless Flag over a Saloo[n]

The American Prohibition Flag

T. P. Flag Co., Pittsburgh, Pa.

Prohibition of Every Evil

The Prohibition Party

s Nation——our Object

Your vote will help may we have it for the ONLY Party
100% loyal to America and without Pro-German votes

Puritan Americanism

a Democracy

★

PROHIBITION FLAG
POSTCARD
CIRCA 1915
USA
PRINTED PAPER
3.5" x 5.5"

The Prohibition Party,
led by the Christian
Temperance group,
used Christian rhetoric
and symbology to
bolster their cause.

★

THE FLAG IN NAT

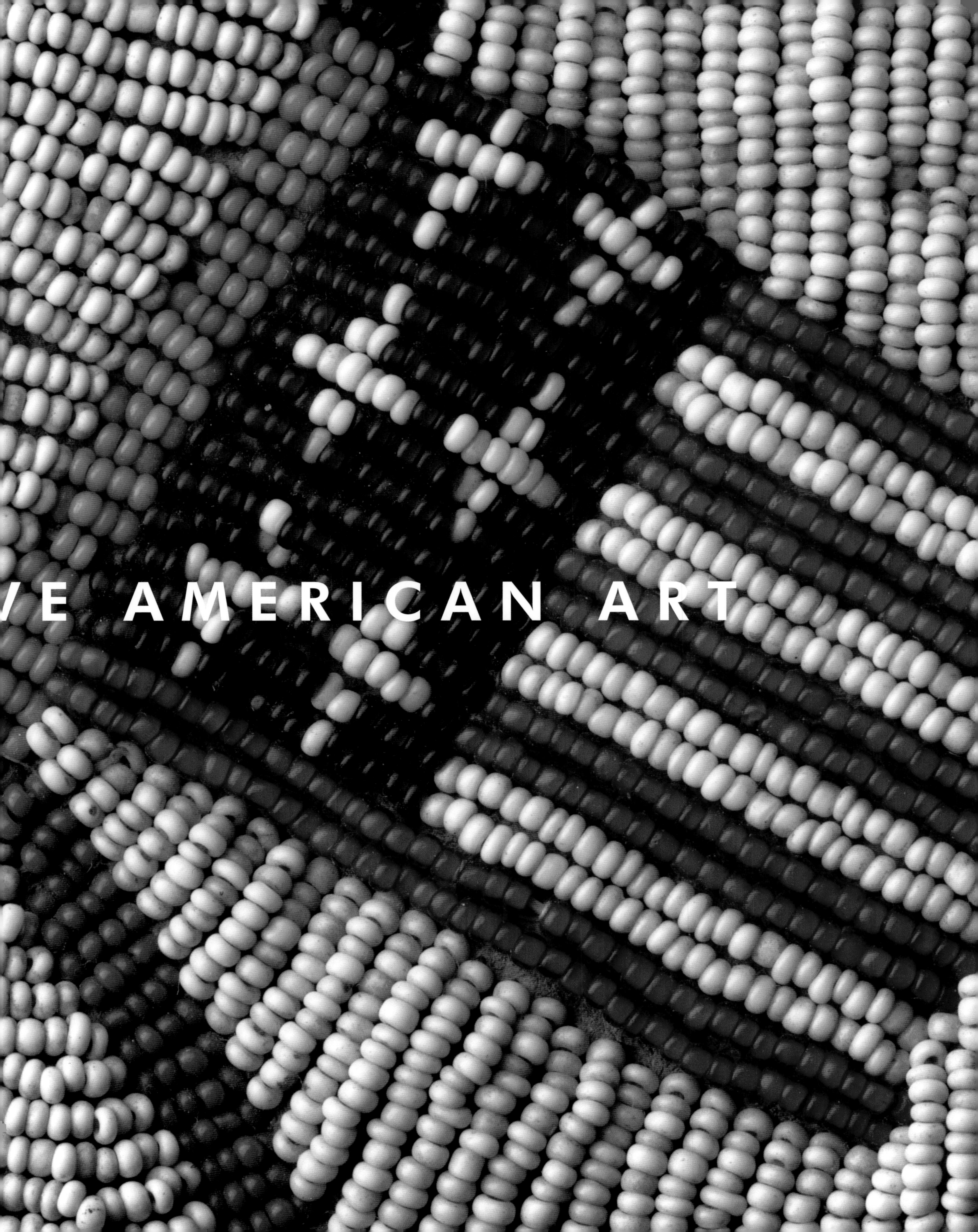
VE AMERICAN ART

★

NAVAJO
CROSS-STAR WEAVING

CIRCA 1980

USA

WOVEN WOOL

22.5" x 28.75"

The difficulty of making
uniform five-pointed stars on a
loom led Navajo weavers to
improvise designs. The cross-
star pattern, representing
the four winds, is a
familiar interpretation.

★

★

IROQUOIS
PLATEAU POUCH

CIRCA 1920

USA

GLASS BEADS AND
LEATHER

12.25" x 5.5"

★

★

WOODLAND INDIANS
PINCUSHION WHIMSY

CIRCA 1920

USA

FELT AND GLASS BEADS

8" x 9.25"

★

★

WOODLAND INDIANS
PINCUSHION WHIMSY

CIRCA 1900

USA

VELVET AND GLASS BEADS

6" x 6"

★

BEADED COIN PURSE

CIRCA 1940

USA

COTTON AND GLASS BEADS

3.38" x 4.5" x .25"

★

Forced to live on reservations with few natural resources, Native Americans struggled to survive by adapting their craft skills to objects that would appeal to the tourist trade. In the early twentieth century, the Woodland Indians created pincushions (sometimes called whimsies), coin purses, and pouches to sell to tourists in the northeastern United States.

★

WOODLAND INDIANS
PINCUSHION WHIMSY
CIRCA 1900
USA
VELVET AND GLASS BEADS
8" x 9.25"

★

★

BEADED FLAG
WAIST POUCH
CIRCA 1950
USA
LEATHER AND
GLASS BEADS
6.5" x 5.75"

★

★

NAVAJO
EIGHTEEN-STAR WEAVING

CIRCA 1945

USA

ANILINE-DYED WOOL

35" x 30"

Beginning as early as the 1870s, Native Americans created weavings for the tourist trade. The American flag was one of the first asymmetrical designs used by Navajo weavers.

★

★

LAKOTA
GAUNTLET GLOVES

CIRCA 1960

USA

GLASS BEADS
AND LEATHER

15.5" x 14.5"

In the early twentieth century, Plains Indians began making gauntlet gloves like those worn by the U.S. Cavalry for commercial sales. The floral-design style was often inspired by images seen in magazines.

★

★

Papoose Doll

Circa 1940

USA

Wood, Beads, Leather,
Cloth, Hair, and Feathers

14.25" x 4" x 4"

Highly collectible today,
children's objects such
as this fully beaded
papoose doll were often
sold as souvenirs.

★

★

CORN HUSK BAG

CIRCA 1900

USA

WOVEN CORN HUSK
AND YARN

8.25" x 7.5"

The Plateau Indians
mastered the art of
making bags by twining
corn husks around a
foundation of native
hemp string. The twine-
weaving technique
complemented the
stylized look of the Stars
and Stripes and eagle.

★

★

Navajo
Fifty-Star Weaving

Circa 1960

USA

Woven Wool

35.75" x 43.5"

★

★

Beaded Fetish

Circa 1980

USA

Beads, Leather,
Tin, and String

4.5" x 2.5" x 1.25"

★

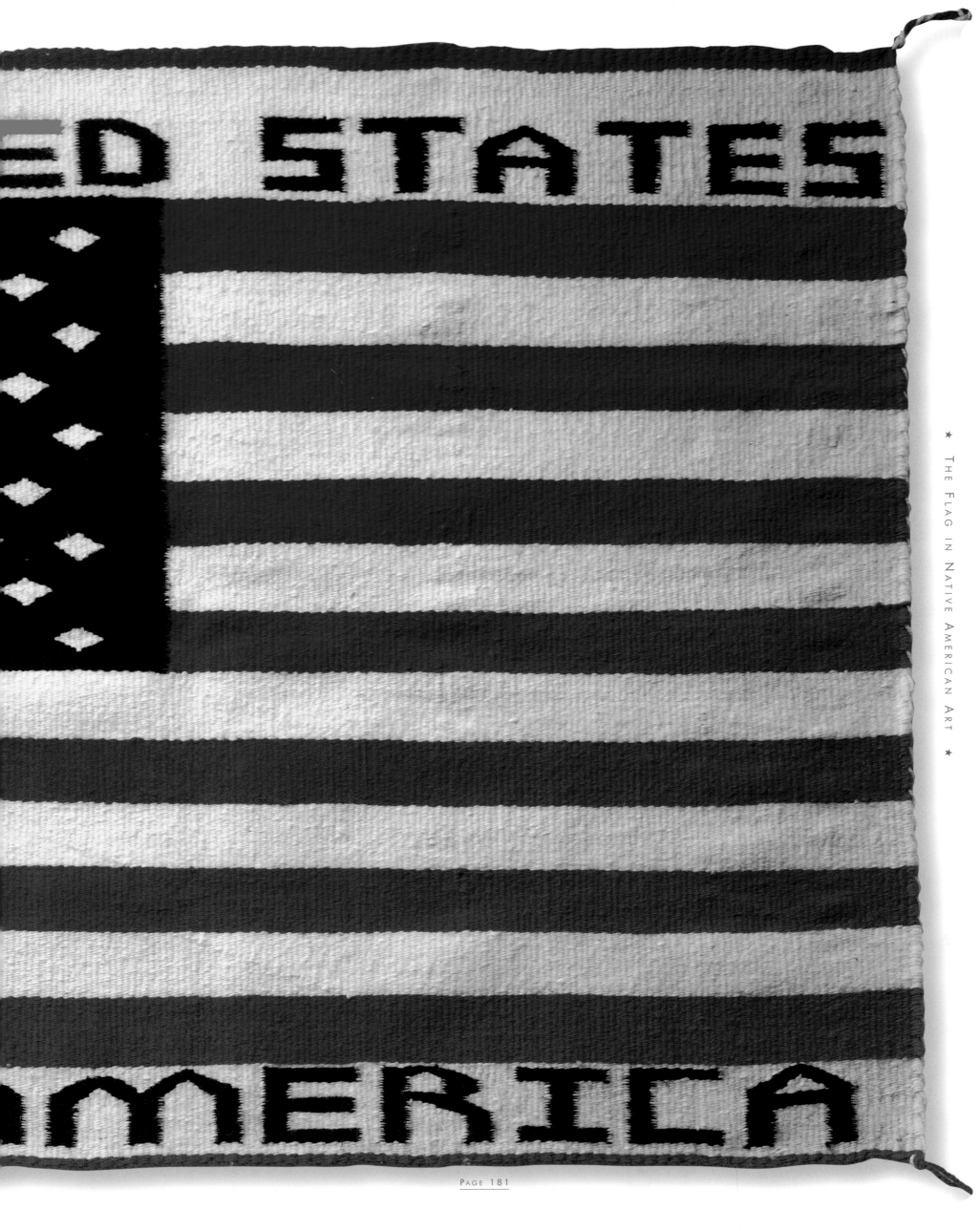

★

RUBIN BASS VIOLIN CASE

1891 / USA / LEATHER, BEADS, METAL, AND WOOD / 10" x 32" x 4.5"

During the Reservation Period in the late nineteenth century, Native Americans were exposed to
many Euro-American ways, some of which they adopted. This elaborate beaded violin case bears the
initials R and B, which stand for the name of its owner, Rubin Bass. The symbolism and
beaded style are representative of the work done by Brule Sioux in South Dakota. "Rubin Bass,
Elk Falls, Feb. 11, 1891" is inscribed in deer hide on the back of the violin case.

★

★

Cheyenne
Flag Moccasins

Circa 1940

USA

Glass Beads and Native
Tanned Hide

11.5" x 4.75" x 3.75"

Traditional Native
American items like
moccasins, armbands, and
breastplates were often
fully beaded by Cheyenne
women. These moccasins
were probably used only
for ceremonial purposes.

★

★

Beaded "H" Belt

Circa 1940

USA

Glass Beads and String

2" x 32"

Created on a loom,
this Lakota beadwork
belt uses the Stars
and Stripes in a way
that seems integral
to the traditional
Native American
geometric pattern.

★

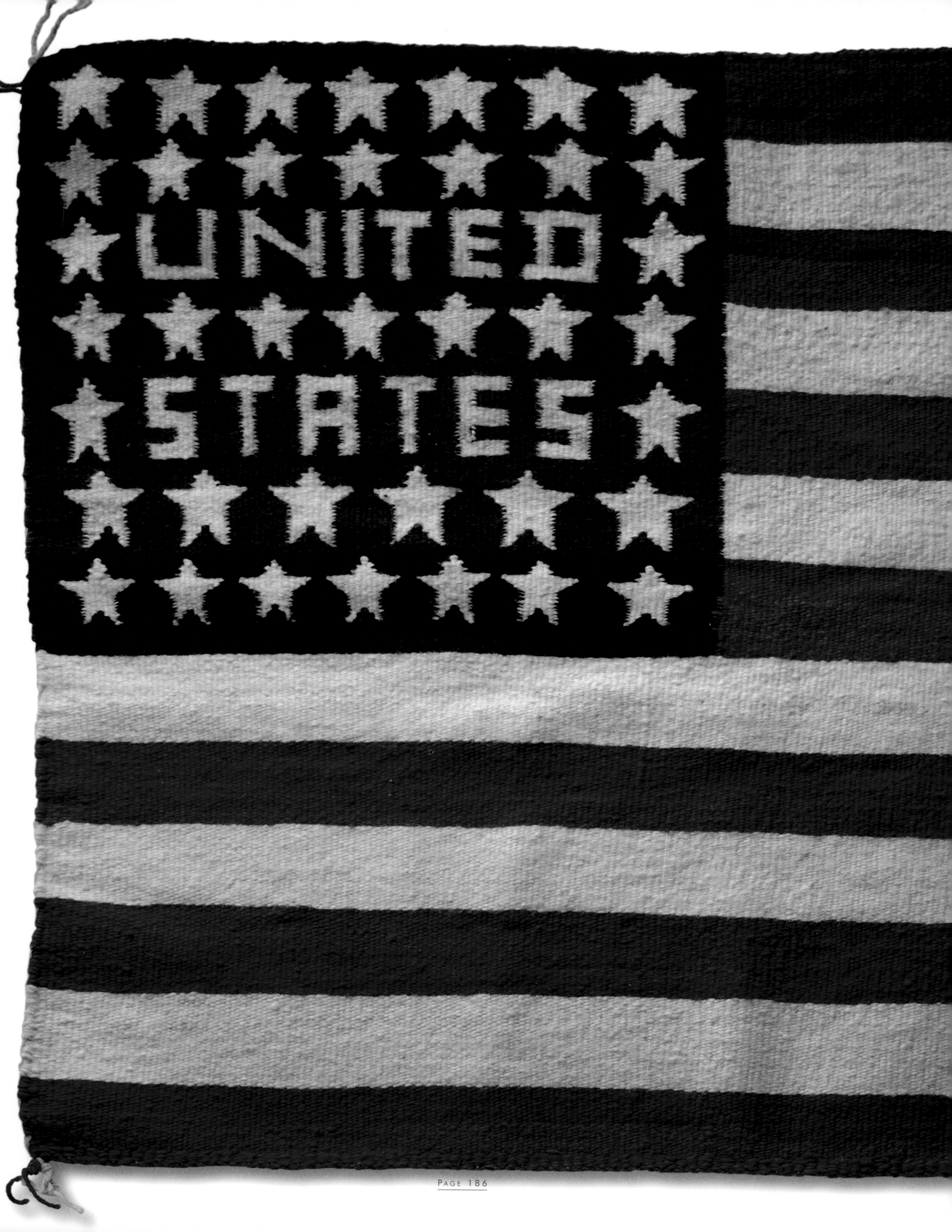
UNITED
STATES

★

NAVAJO
"UNITED STATES"
WEAVING
1959
USA
WOVEN WOOL
30" x 38.5"

★

★

LAKOTA
MOCCASINS
CIRCA 1960
USA
GLASS BEADS
AND DEER HIDE
10" x 3.75" x 3.5"

★

★

NAVAJO
CHEVROLET WEAVING

1945

USA

WOVEN WOOL

29" x 44"

Found at the Albuquerque
"Cowboy and Indian"
antiques show, this forty-
eight-star flag weaving
originally hung in a
Gallup, New Mexico,
Navajo Chevrolet
dealership.

★

★

QUILL KNIFE SHEATH

CIRCA 1910

USA

DYED PORCUPINE
QUILLS AND LEATHER

10" x 13"

In the late nineteenth
century, the Lakota
began making beaded
and quilled items with
patriotic designs. Such
decorated items, like
this knife sheath, were
used both by the local
tribes for ceremonies
and sold to tourists.

★

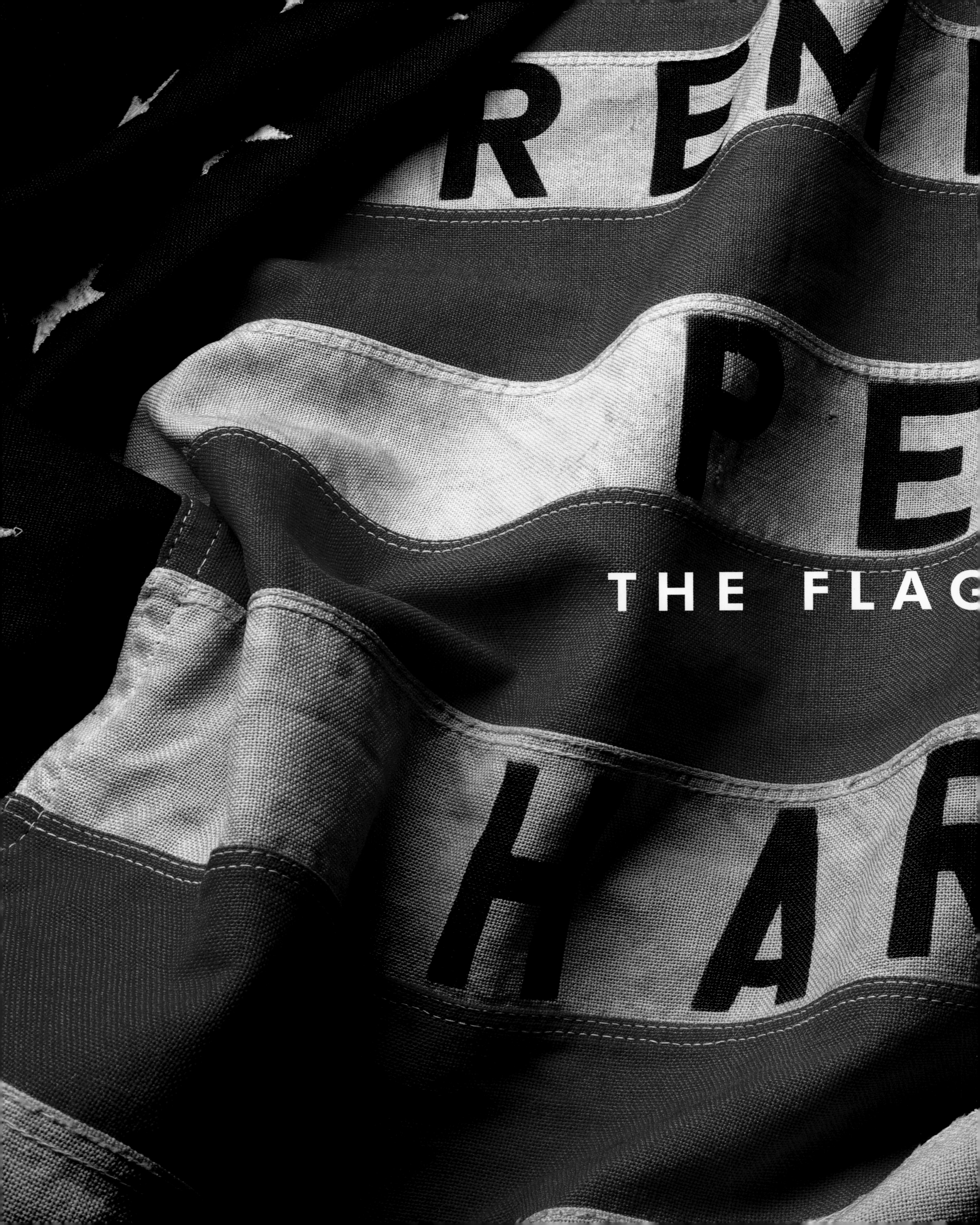
THE FLAG

AT WAR

"OVER THE TOP"
POSTER

CIRCA 1917

USA

LETTERPRESS ON PAPER

30" X 19.5"

Sidney Riesenberg, one
of the country's great
illustrators during World
War I, communicated
the urgency of the Third
Liberty Bond drive
through the desperate
look of a young soldier
gripping the flag.

★

★

GENERAL MACARTHUR
COIN BANK

WORLD WAR II ERA

USA

PRINTED PAPER AND GLASS

7" X 11" X .75"

General MacArthur, often
accused of having a larger
public relations staff than
military staff, is shown
here on a Save for Victory
Bank. When the bank was
full, the saver would
dutifully buy a war bond
with the contents.

★

★

"GIVE IT YOUR BEST!"
POSTER

1942

USA

PRINTED PAPER

28" x 40"

GIVE IT YOUR BEST!

During World War II,
the U.S. Office for
Emergency Management
commissioned several
of the nation's leading
designers and artists
to create posters
encouraging people to
support the war effort.
This poster by Charles
Coiner was reproduced
in four sizes for display
in different public spaces.
It was even sold as a
two-inch stick-on "poster
stamp" (shown above).

★

GIVE IT

DIVISION OF INFORMATION
OFFICE FOR EMERGENCY MANAGEMENT
WASHINGTON, D. C.
⊕ U. S. GOVERNMENT PRINTING OFFICE : 1942—O-455950

Weather-vane and lightening-rod
manufacturers found the
American flag a popular subject
during World War II. (The word
vane comes from the Anglo-Saxon
word *fane*, meaning "flag.")
The holes in some of the stars
shown here were made by
farmboys using the fixtures for
target practice. This collection
combines World War II printed-tin
flags with a World War I copper
doughboy holding a painted flag.

★ FLAG LIGHTNING ROD

★ DOUGHBOY WEATHER VANE

★ FLAG LIGHTNING ROD

★

WORLD WAR II
PATRIOTIC PILLOW COVER

CIRCA 1942

USA

PRINTED SILK

19" x 19" x 9"

During World War II, a
popular souvenir among
military personnel was the
satin pillowcase printed
with sentimental verse and
patriotic pictures. The
decorative pillowcases
were easy to mail home,
and parents proudly
displayed them in their
parlors to show they had
sons serving overseas.

★

COREA
1871
BY
BATT

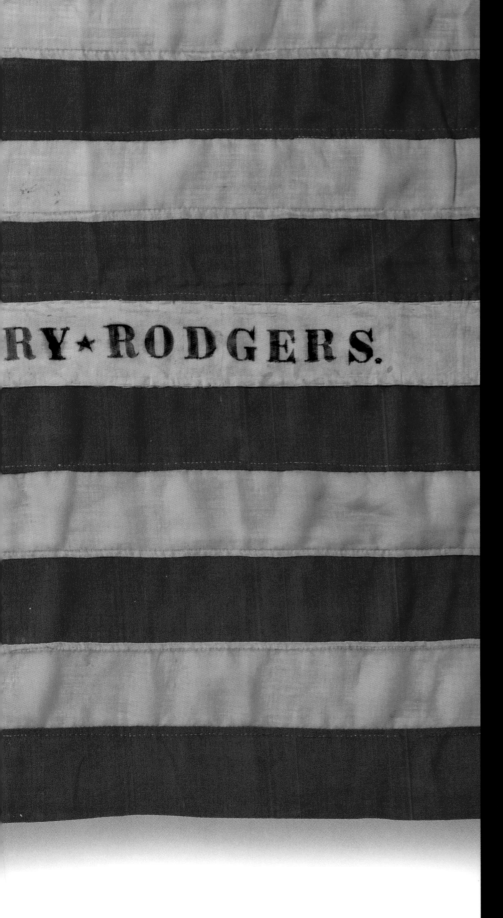

LAND, OR BY SEA!

RY ★ RODGERS.

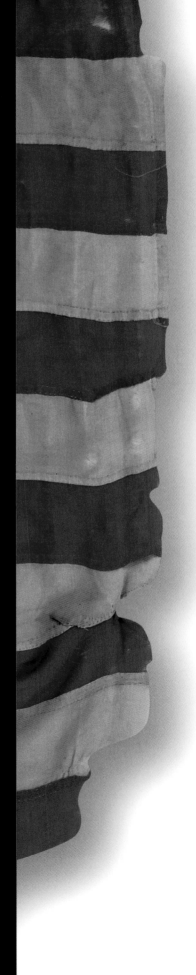

★

RODGERS'S BATTLE FLAG

This flag flew on ships commanded by Admiral John Rodgers during the Civil War and the Korean conflict of 1871. Originally issued to the North Atlantic Blockading Squadron in 1860, the banner first saw action in 1861, when an ironclad ship, commanded by then-Captain Rodgers, was attacked by Confederate troops who fired cannons down onto the ship from a bluff above the James River. Seventy percent of the crew were killed or wounded, but Rodgers did not withdraw from action until his vessel was riddled with holes and the engine was disabled. For his bravery, Rodgers was promoted to rear admiral and presented with the battle-scarred flag. In 1871, Admiral Rodgers was put in command of the Asiatic Fleet, which landed one thousand men on the shores of Korea (Corea). Again, the flag witnessed several conflicts. After the signing of a treaty with Korea, Admiral Rodgers presented the flag to the lieutenant who had risked his life rescuing it during the storming of a fort on the Seoul River.

★

★

"USA BONDS"
POSTER
1918
USA
PRINTED PAPER
30" x 19.5"

German immigrant
Joseph Leyendecker, best
known for his *Saturday
Evening Post* covers and
as the illustrator for the
debonair Arrow Collar
Man, produced this
poster, one of the most
famous of World War I.

★

★

CIVIL WAR FLAG
1865
USA
PRINTED COTTON
16" x 25"

The veterans group
from the 71st New York
Volunteer Infantry
imprinted the battles it
fought during the Civil
War on a thirty-five-star,
double-wreath flag.

★

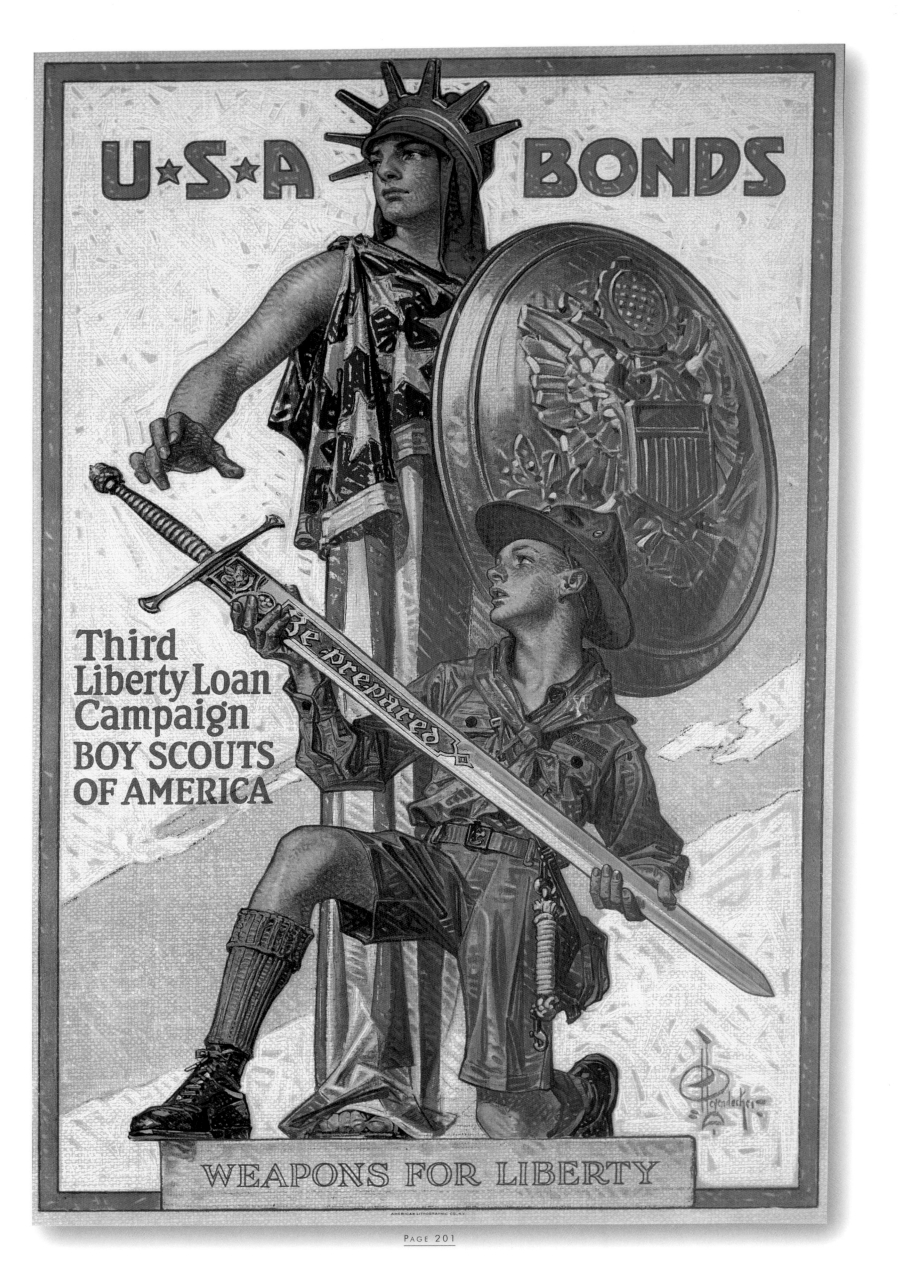

★

SPANISH-AMERICAN WAR
VETERANS HONOR MEDAL

1902

USA

BRONZE WITH SILK RIBBON

4.5" X 1.75"

The American press
whipped the nation into
a war frenzy after the
USS *Maine* was sunk in
Cuba's Havana harbor,
leaving 260 dead. Fighting
in the Spanish-American
War of 1898 lasted only
four months. Some 460
Americans lost their lives
in battle and another
5,200 succumbed to
tropical diseases.

★

★

SHANGHAI
PICTURE FRAME

1945

CHINA

CARVED AND PAINTED
WOOD AND GLASS

13" X 9.25" X .75"

At the end of World
War II, Chinese artisans
in the Asiatic theater
of action did a brisk
business in producing
picture frames for
soldiers and sailors
who wished to send
their photographs
home to loved ones.

★

"REMEMBER PEARL HARBOR"
COMMEMORATIVE BOX

CIRCA 1942

USA

PRINTED METAL AND GLASS

11" x 9.25" x .75"

Printed vertical panels
present three distinct
images when viewed from
different angles.

★

Soldiers and loved ones,
from both sides of
the war, expressed belief
in their cause through
hundreds of different
patriotic images printed
on envelopes.

★

★

THE FLAG AT WAR

★

OUR FLAG ★ YOUR FLAG
VICTORIOUS
IN A THOUSAND
BATTLES
HERE'S TO ANOTHER VICTORY

HERE'S TO OUR
GLORIOUS
FLAG
UNTARNISHED, UNSULLIED
UNBEATEN

STARS and STRIPES
Fearlessly
Floating
for
HUMANITY & DEMOCRACY

FLAG
OF THE
FREE
★
FIGHT TO KEEP IT FREE

OUR FLAG
Champion
of the
oppressed
♥
LIBERTY FOREVER

STAND BY
YOUR
COLORS
&
YOUR COLORS WILL STAND BY YOU

★

PATRIOTIC POSTCARDS

WORLD WAR I ERA

USA

PRINTED PAPER

3.5" x 5.5"

Before E-mail and
telephones, postcards
were a popular way
of keeping in touch.
During World War I,
postcard sets often
featured encouraging
patriotic slogans.

★

★ CAMP BEALE POSTCARD ★

★ SPANISH-AMERICAN WAR NEEDLE CONTAINER ★

Our Flag
and
Our Hero

GENERAL MacARTHUR

★ U.S. NAVY EMBLEM ★   ★ PERFUME POSTCARD ★

★ PEARL HARBOR BUTTON ★

Every war produced its share of memorabilia, from needle tins and perfumed cards to wall calendars and banners.

★ GENERAL MACARTHUR PENNANT ★

★ GENERAL PERSHING POSTCARD ★

★ ADMIRAL DEWEY PIN ★

★ THE FLAG AT WAR ★

1945 JANUARY 1945

Sun.	Mon.	Tue.	Wed.	Thu.	Fri.	Sat.
L.Q. 6th						
	1	2	3	4	5	6
7	8	9	10	11	12	13
14	15	16	17	18	19	20
21	22	23	24	25	26	27
28	29	30	31	N.M. 14th	F.Q. 20th	F.M. 28th

COPR. C. MOSS 1944

OUR HERO

★ ADMIRAL DEWEY WHISKEY FLASK ★

★ STATUE OF LIBERTY CALENDAR ★

"BEFORE SUNSET"

POSTER

1917

USA

PRINTED PAPER

30" x 20"

In 1917, as World War I raged on in Europe, the U.S. government urgently sought to raise more funds to support the war effort. This poster by Eugenie Deland metaphorically pleads for people to buy war bonds before the sun sets on American liberties.

ARMY AND NAVY

NEEDLE BOOKS

1898

GERMANY

PRINTED PAPER

2.75" x 4.75"

Between acts of heroism, Spanish-American War soldiers and sailors performed such mundane personal chores as darning and mending their uniforms.

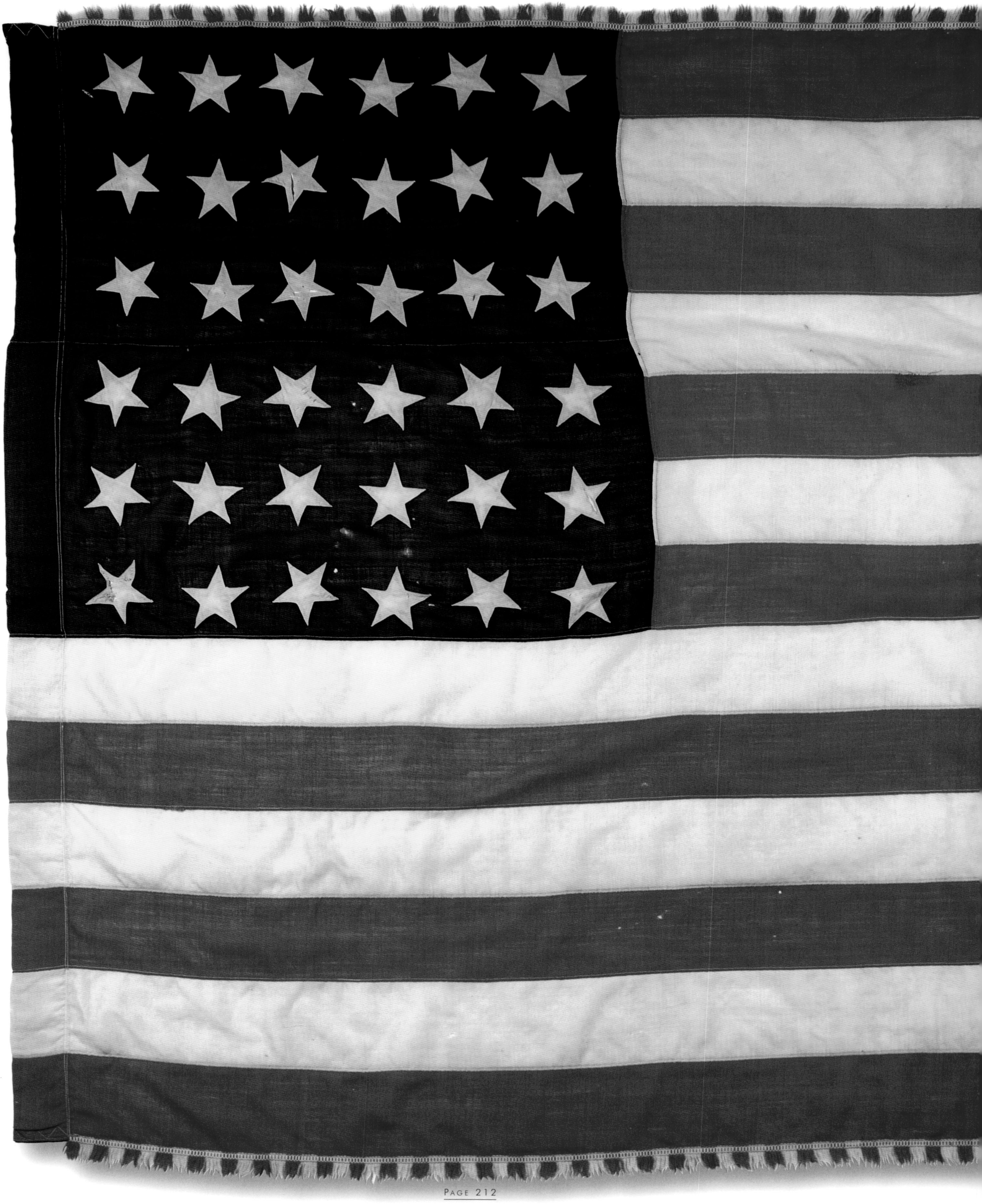

★

THIRTY-SIX-STAR FLAG

CIRCA 1865

USA

WOOL BUNTING WITH
COTTON STARS

64" X 72"

Toward the close of the
Civil War, a high-ranking
Union officer commis-
sioned the making of this
artillery battery flag.

★

★

GULF WAR BLOOD CHIT

1991

USA

PRINTED NYLON

10.5" X 8.5"

Beginning in World War II
American fighter pilots
started carrying these
so-called blood chits
when flying into enemy
territory. Usually sewn
inside a flight jacket, the
multilanguage message
explains the carrier is an
American and offers
a reward to anyone
providing safe passage.

★

★

"FLAG OF FREEDOM"
POSTER

1917

USA

PRINTED PAPER

15.75" x 11.75"

This World War I rallying poster is rife with patriotic symbolism: soldiers marching resolutely off to war with the Statue of Liberty in the distance, and an Army Corps nurse standing on the foundation of the Liberty Bell while raising the banner of freedom.

★

★

"A DAUGHTER OF THE REGIMENT"

CIVIL WAR ERA

USA

LITHOGRAPH ON PAPER

8.25" x 6"

★

FLAG of FREEDOM

★ "REMEMBER PEARL HARBOR" FLAG / 1942 / USA / PRINTED CLOTH / 30" x 57" ★

★ At liberty bond rallies during World War II, glamorous movie stars often auctioned off flags such as this one to raise funds for the war effort. ★

Using a photo process
introduced during World
War I, decorative frames
with portraits were
printed as a single
celluloid image. The
unbreakable frames
were easy to send back
to families at home.

★

★ THE FLAG AT WAR ★

FIELD MARSHAL SIR DOUGLAS HAIG   MARSHAL FERDINAND FOCH   GENERAL JOHN J. PERSHING   GENERAL ARMANDO DIAZ

The Great Victory Generals of the World

★

"THE GREAT VICTORY
GENERALS OF THE WORLD"
COMMEMORATIVE PLACARD

1919

USA

PRINTED PAPER

11.25" x 14.75"

★

★ Thirteen-Star Post–Civil War Flag / Circa 1866 / USA / Wool / 40″ x 72″ ★

This tattered and mended thirteen-star flag was made by Union general Benjamin "the Beast" Butler,

who started a bunting-and-flags business following the Civil War.

A Chronological History

The American flag has changed frequently and dramatically since the Continental Congress resolved on June 14, 1777 "that the flag of the United States be thirteen stripes, alternate red and white; that the Union be thirteen stars, white in a blue field representing a new constellation." The vague wording left much room for graphic interpretation, encouraged further by two Congressional acts. In 1795, Congress decreed that a single star and single stripe be added whenever a new stated joined the Union. In 1818, Congress changed its mind, reverting back to thirteen horizontal stripes, alternating red and white, to symbolize the original colonies, with each state represented by a single star. The new star would be added on the Fourth of July following a state's admission to the Union. In 1912, Congress finally legislated official graphic standards for how the flag must appear. Presented here is a chronology of state admissions and one example of how the flag was graphically interpreted at that time.

June 14, 1777 (13 stars)

Delaware

Pennsylvania

New Jersey

Georgia

Connecticut

Massachusetts

Maryland

South Carolina

New Hampshire

Virginia

New York

North Carolina

Rhode Island

★

President Serving under the Flag

George Washington

May 1, 1795 (15 stars)

Vermont

Kentucky

★

Presidents Serving under the Flag

George Washington

John Adams, Thomas Jefferson

James Madison, James Monroe

July 4, 1836 (25 stars)

Arkansas

★

Presidents Serving under the Flag

Andrew Jackson

Martin Van Buren

July 4, 1848 (30 stars)

Wisconsin

★

Presidents Serving under the Flag

James K. Polk

Zachary Taylor

Millard Fillmore

July 4, 1851 (31 stars)

California

★

Presidents Serving under the Flag

Millard Fillmore

Franklin Pierce

James Buchanan

July 4, 1858 (32 stars)

Minnesota

★

President Serving under the Flag

James Buchanan

July 4, 1859 (33 stars)

Oregon

★

Presidents Serving under the Flag

James Buchanan

Abraham Lincoln

July 4, 1877 (38 stars)

Colorado

★

Presidents Serving under the Flag

Rutherford B. Hayes, James Garfield

Chester Alan Arthur, Grover Cleveland

Benjamin Harrison

July 4, 1890 (43 stars)

North Dakota

South Dakota

Montana

Washington

Idaho

★

President Serving under the Flag

Benjamin Harrison

July 4, 1891 (44 stars)

Wyoming

★

Presidents Serving under the Flag

Benjamin Harrison

Grover Cleveland

July 4, 1896 (45 stars)

Utah

★

Presidents Serving under the Flag

Grover Cleveland

William McKinley

Theodore Roosevelt

April 13, 1818 (20 stars)

Tennessee, Ohio

Louisiana, Indiana

Mississippi

★

President Serving under the Flag

James Monroe

July 4, 1819 (21 stars)

Illinois

★

President Serving under the Flag

James Monroe

July 4, 1820 (23 stars)

Alabama

Maine

★

President Serving under the Flag

James Monroe

July 4, 1822 (24 stars)

Missouri

★

Presidents Serving under the Flag

James Monroe

John Quincy Adams

Andrew Jackson

July 4, 1837 (26 stars)

Michigan

★

Presidents Serving under the Flag

Martin Van Buren

William Henry Harrison

John Tyler

James K. Polk

July 4, 1845 (27 stars)

Florida

★

President Serving under the Flag

James K. Polk

July 4, 1846 (28 stars)

Texas

★

President Serving under the Flag

James K. Polk

July 4, 1847 (29 stars)

Iowa

★

President Serving under the Flag

James K. Polk

July 4, 1861 (34 stars)

Kansas

★

President Serving under the Flag

Abraham Lincoln

July 4, 1863 (35 stars)

West Virginia

★

Presidents Serving under the Flag

Abraham Lincoln

Andrew Johnson

July 4, 1865 (36 stars)

Nevada

★

President Serving under the Flag

Andrew Johnson

July 4, 1867 (37 stars)

Nebraska

★

Presidents Serving under the Flag

Andrew Johnson

Ulysses S. Grant

Rutherford B. Hayes

July 4, 1908 (46 stars)

Oklahoma

★

Presidents Serving under the Flag

Theodore Roosevelt

William Howard Taft

July 4, 1912 (48 stars)

New Mexico

Arizona

★

Presidents Serving under the Flag

William Howard Taft, Woodrow Wilson

Warren G. Harding, Calvin Coolidge

Herbert Hoover, Franklin D. Roosevelt

Harry S. Truman, Dwight D. Eisenhower

July 4, 1959 (49 stars)

Alaska

★

President Serving under the Flag

Dwight D. Eisenhower

July 4, 1960 (50 stars)

Hawaii

★

Presidents Serving under the Flag

Dwight D. Eisenhower, John F. Kennedy

Lyndon Johnson, Richard Nixon

Gerald Ford, Jimmy Carter

Ronald Reagan, George H. W. Bush

William Clinton, George W. Bush

★ A CHRONOLOGICAL HISTORY ★

Special Thanks

A special thanks to my collaborators Delphine Hirasuna and Terry Heffernan, whose generous spirit and support made this book possible. Additional thanks for photography to Bob Esparza, John South, and Dan Goldberg. I'd also like to thank Craig McClain, Dr. Jeffery Kenneth Kohn, Susan Parrish, and Julia Moed, who have made collecting fun. Additional thanks to my sister, Gretchen Kirk, for sharing our family heirloom. And to my wife, Linda, and son, Christopher, for enduring all the late nights and long weekends without complaint. To my design colleagues Shelby Carr, Takayo Muroga, and Karen Montgomery, for getting it done. And, of course, to Kirsty Melville and Aaron Wehner, whose enthusiasm for the book got it launched.

Credits

© 2001 by Kit Hinrichs and Delphine Hirasuna

Photography © 2001 by Terry Heffernan

A Kirsty Melville Book

Ten Speed Press P.O. Box 7123 Berkeley, California 94707 www.tenspeed.com

Distributed in Australia by Simon and Schuster Australia, in Canada by Ten Speed Press Canada, in New Zealand by Southern Publishers Group, in South Africa by Real Books, in Southeast Asia by Berkeley Books, and in the United Kingdom and Europe by Airlift Book Company.

Design by Kit Hinrichs/Pentagram

Design Associate: Shelby Carr/Pentagram

Photography by Terry Heffernan

Library of Congress Cataloging-in-Publication Data on file with publisher

Printed in China

4 5 6 7 8 9 10 — 05 04 03 02

Limited slipcase edition ISBN 1-58008-312-9

Cloth edition ISBN 1-58008-240-8

I Pledge Alle
Flag of the
of America,
Republic fo
Stands, One
God, Indiv
Liberty and J